From the Publisher

Here is a modern edition of 1865's *The Unjust Judge.*

The "unjust judge" is Roger B. Taney, fifth U.S. chief justice. He who was the author of the decision in the *Dred Scott* case.

The decision issued in March 1857. (It was two days after Buchanan's inauguration.) From a segment of politicians, lawyers, commentators, clergy and others, the pushback was immediate and vociferous. Not until after Taney's death in office in October 1864 did there appear the definitive rebuttal. With a scathing personal attack on Taney. This was the pamphlet *The Unjust Judge.* It is fierce, frank, unrestrained, devastating, scholarly, insightful, inspiring, eloquent, elegant and flamboyant.

It was published anonymously. Dispositive evidence of who the author is has not been advanced. The evident consensus is that it is most likely that the author is Charles Sumner, senator from Massachusetts. (See note facing the photograph of Sumner below.)

(It is beyond astonishing that Taney was permitted to continue in office in the face of the fatal damage he had by *Dred Scott* wrecked upon the Constitution. Even more so in the face of the consequent Civil War. As to which, as a Southerner with a Southern mindset and Southern sympathies, he constituted a sympathizer of the enemy. To conduct a war with as chief justice an enemy sympathizer—a potential agent of the enemy—was an absurdity.)

With this Edgy® edition, the publisher is pleased to make this work readily accessible to the history student and to the general reader. Today is marked by ever-increasing interest in slavery and race. There is no doubt, then, that this work is certain to claim ever-increasing attention.

This edition contains the entire text of the original.

So that this edition support citations to the original, the original page numbers are inserted, in brackets, in the text. The text immediately following an original number is the text that appears at the top of the original page with that number.

Paragraphs that are, to the modern reader, forbiddingly intimidating in their gargantuan length, are divided. A place where this is done, at a logical point, is indicated by a small paragraph symbol.

The reader just now making the acquaintance of Taney should be aware that the name is pronounced "Tawny"—like the color. There is irony in this. That is, that the name of history's greatest defender of Whiteness is pronounced as is a name of species of Brownness.

—John Wirth, Publisher, Edgy books from grawlix®

Front Cover

"Roger B. Taney: Wanted for Judicial Malfeasance"

BACKGROUND GRAPHIC (OF A NAILED-UP BLANK WANTED POSTER): GRAFISSIMO/GETTY IMAGES PHOTO: ALAMY
FONT: WG_WANTED.TTF / TITLE OF FONT: "UNTITLED" / NATHAN BROWN/WEGRAPHICS SEPARATOR: GARY GODBY/EPHEMERA FONTS CO.

THE UNJUST JUDGE

THE UNJUST JUDGE:

ROGER B. TANEY

5th Chief Justice of the United States

Charles Sumner

Edgy

The new edition of Unjust Judge
is for Marcia Flammonde
for your indulgent presence and excellent food

Slavery is not a part of the history of the United States.
Slavery *is* the history of the United States.

—John Wirth

The cover of the original pamphlet. As seen, the pamphlet was self-published and privately printed in New York City. It was copyrighted in 1865 as an anonymous work, by the printer, Baker & Godwin. The Copyright Office permitted—and permits—copyright with the author kept anonymous.

THE UNJUST JUDGE.

A MEMORIAL

OF

ROGER BROOKE TANEY,

LATE

CHIEF JUSTICE OF THE UNITED STATES.

"For with what judgment ye judge, ye shall be judged; and with what measure ye mete, it shall be measured to you again."—MATT. VII. 1, 2.

NEW YORK:
BAKER & GODWIN, PRINTERS,
PRINTING-HOUSE SQUARE, OPP. CITY HALL.
1865.

Charles Sumner (1811-1874) photographed ca. 1865. In Senate 1851-1874.

The presumed author of the anonymous *Unjust Judge*. Republican senator and avowed and militant abolitionist. He who in 1856 was assaulted by a congressman from South Carolina.

See pp. 40-46 for the view taken of South Carolina and of John C. Calhoun, senator from that state.

Sumner's opinion of Taney was well known. In 1865 he objected to Congress commissioning a bust of Taney for display in the Capitol. He said in the Senate, "I speak what cannot be denied when I declare that the opinion of the Chief Justice in the case of Dred Scott was more thoroughly abominable than anything of the kind in the history of courts."

See p. 80 for similar language.

Rhetoric—of which Sumner was, it would be hard to dispute, in his time the preeminent master—has in its kit the tool of sarcasm. The author's huge sarcasm of casting his "notice" as a "memorial" cannot not be recognized.

MATHEW BRADY/LIBRARY OF CONGRESS HEALED IMAGE BY JOHN WIRTH

vation and experience of its workings and results. The practice of law in a slave State forced him to ascertain the rights of Slavery under the law, and by consequence, the rights of Freedom in its presence. The conclusions of his mind and conscience upon the whole matter, when he was equally removed from the fatuity of old age, and the thoughtlessness of youth, are very clearly developed by an incident in his professional life.

In 1818, when he had reached the age at which, it is said, a man is "wise, if ever," he defended Rev. Jacob Gruber, a Methodist minister, indicted under the slave laws of Maryland, for having preached a sermon, designed, as was charged, to incite slaves to disorder. It is impossible, even at this distance of time, to read and not admire the boldness and dignity of that defense.

The prosecution failed signally to prove the intent necessary to constitute the statutory crime, and the acquittal of the accused became inevitable. The indignant scorn with which Mr. Taney rejected that mode of escape for his client, is a fine exhibition of that temper of mind. "But the reverend gentleman," said he, "merits a defense on very different principles. The counsel to whom he has confided his cause cannot content themselves with a cold and reluctant acquittal, and abandon Mr. Gruber, without defense, to all the obloquy and reproach which his enemies have industriously and most unjustly heaped upon him. We cannot consent to buy his safety, by yielding to passion, prejudice and avarice, the control of future discussions on this great and important question. He must not surrender up the civil and religious rights secured to him, in common with **[9]**others, by the Constitution of this most favored nation.¶

"Mr. Gruber feels that it is clue to his own character, to the station he fills, to the respectable society of Christians in which he is a minister of the Gospel, not only to defend himself from this prosecution, but also to avow and vindicate here, the principles he maintained in his sermon. There is no law that forbids us to speak of Slavery as we think of it. Any man has a right to publish

Any such use would be in violation of every code of morals, christian or pagan, of which we have any account. It would justify France in declaring she would never have abetted the Revolution; Holland that she would not have loaned us money; other powers that they would not have remained neutral; England that she never would have made peace, had the aims of the American people been less noble than they declared. We commit to the dungeon, and very properly, the rogue who obtains goods or money by kindred means; but where is there an abyss wide enough and deep enough to receive a nation which would obtain its independence under false pretenses? **[15]**What measure of contempt can be equal to the deserts of those misleaders of the people, who counsel national dishonesty because there is no tribunal to punish an offender of so gigantic proportions? The man who can himself consent to it, or advise others to do it, because no grand jury can indict nor petit jury convict the nation of fraud, is a public enemy, and upon the first temptation will discover, that he is as destitute of personal honesty as of public virtue.

When Mr. Taney. stood in the court-house at Frederick and insisted "on the principles contained in that venerated instrument," he revealed his own consciousness, and warned us, that they cannot be surrendered without grave danger to the most precious rights of citizenship. However much the good name of the nation might suffer from such an act, the rights of American citizens would suffer more. To restore the Declaration to its first place in the thoughts and hearts of the American people, would be a more valuable service than to add a continent to their jurisdiction. It is our first, as it is our most glorious, deed. It is a written instrument—executed, recorded, and published in an hour of the peril and the honesty of the country. It is older than the Constitution, beyond which the American memory seems no longer to run. It is the first lien upon the "sacred honor" and good faith of the American people. Except by defiant fraud, no subsequent incumbrance can take precedence of it.

Every departure of our people from the conditions, and

ments are instituted among men." This committed the American people on two points—one in regard to the natural rights of man, the other as to the true object of government—it was optional with all other people to adopt those views or not.¶

While the war for independence existed, *"in hoc signo vinces"* flashed from the Declaration as cheerily as it would have from a Constitution; and as properly, perhaps, seeing the purpose of the struggle was rather to acquire, than to secure, the rights in question. But war is not the normal condition of any people, not even the Ishmaelites, and when that strife was composed by concession of the rights claimed, the thoughts of men turned naturally towards laws and regulations adapted to secure the rights established, and provide for the enjoyment of them in a condition of peace, which it was hoped would be perpetual.¶

The Constitution came from the necessities of the condition of peace, intensified by the failure of the scheme of the Confederation; and though it claimed less, it accomplished more than the Declaration itself. The one *claimed* for all men, everywhere, the precise rights that the other *secured* to all men within its jurisdiction—that is, within the territorial sovereignty of the United States. The Declaration, in a legal and technical sense, secured nobody; the Constitution secured everybody within the boundaries of its power. The Declaration made a claim, the war of the Revolution enforced it, and the Constitution secured the benefits of it to the American people.¶

The claim was for Liberty, the men of the Revolution fought for Liberty, and the Constitution was ordained to "secure the blessings of Liberty;" therefore any construction of it, opposed to that object, must be unjust, and nothing unjust can ever be sound. If the letter be pronounced fatal, judicially, the duty **[22]**is to apply the remedy, thoughtfully provided for such a contingency by the instrument itself—amendment. In no event are we to cloak, by affected deference to mooted constitutional requirements, practical repudiation of the fundamental principles con-

to the Framers, that they were transcending but little the then almost universal practice of imprisonment for debt.¶

Be that as it may, the slaveholder or hunter, coming into the presence of the Federal judiciary, was required to conceal his actual relation to his chattel, in order to entitle himself to such use of its power as this melancholy provision tolerated. He must claim a "person, held to service or labor in one State, under the laws thereof," wherefrom he had escaped. His owing "service or labor," operated no more to destroy his personality [personalty], in the contemplation of the Constitution, than a debt, due in money, from the Chief Justice, would, to degrade that high functionary to chattelhood.¶

That Slavery, even under the disguise of manhood, might never attain to any better foundation or more extended jurisdiction than could be eliminated from the laws of a single State, the manner in which debtors of the class in question should he held, was prescribed by the Con-**[28]**stitution to be, "in one State, under the laws thereof." This, of course, excluded all other modes of holding, and made the provision useless to any slavery authorized by the laws of more States than one or by the laws of the United States.

Neither the Constitution, nor the Framers, are responsible for the iniquities and barbarities that have been perpetrated under cover of this provision. The guilt of them is our own; and so is the penalty, as our condition this day abundantly proves.¶

Neither laws made under it, nor adjudications made under them, have ever conformed to the provision in letter or spirit. Every one of them has been in violation of it and other important constitutional guarantees; all of them matters of solemn agreement between rival powers that settled thus a contested supremacy. In every case of appeal to its arbitrament, the shield of the Constitution has been placed before the assailant of constitutional right and liberty; and the "life, liberty and property" of persons have been taken "without due process of law." The People, the

casion than quarrels on the race-course, in the cock-pit, or at the gaming table.¶

If Sumter had been garrisoned by a foreign enemy, not a gun would have been trained upon it by the Gascons of the State; but held by fellow-citizens, in the uniform of Freedom, for the defence of public liberty, the mark was irresistibly tempting. South Carolina, like Cain, sheds none but fraternal blood.

[34]The moral and social condition of South Carolina has always been propitious to the growth and culture of such principles as Mr. Calhoun finally developed, but never genial to the production of such intellect and manners as he certainly possessed. In the walks of private life he was temperate, decorous and respectable, to a degree most unusual among his class. He seems to have been free from even the small vices that obtain in communities of stricter morality than that in which he lived. As husband, father, friend and neighbor, he lived a long life without reproach. In such relations it is delightful to contemplate him. As a public man, however, his instincts and habits were those of an African slave-trader; avoiding the cruisers of Freedom at sea, and her beacon lights on land, intent only upon running a cargo of slaves into some friendly cove, under cover of darkness. He always steered by the compass of slavery.¶

That institution, the natural enemy of the human race, under the increasing illumination of the public mind and conscience during the first half of this century, became more and more odious year by year. Conscious of this persistent augmentation of the contempt and dislike of the civilized world, like most outlaws, repelling alike shame and repentance, it addressed itself to a more diligent watching for opportunities of revenge and reprisal. Savagely vindictive in temper, unscrupulous in regard to means, and infatuated in respect to its own force, it proceeded to devise schemes and policies that might enable it to withstand the moral power of the world, and, if need be, the physical also.¶

In this enterprise Mr. Calhoun, who possessed the subtlest

possession of an absolute right "to prevent the increase of Slavery;" which, beyond all doubt, was, at the time of the grant, understood to include abolishing it altogether. It was claimed and granted in the Convention.¶

Roger Sherman's statement, that *"the States now possessed the right and the public good did not require it to be taken away,"* was distinctly met and controverted. If the point had not been raised, the liberal side of the question would still prevail on other grounds, but having been raised, specifically, and decided as it was, the proposition stands upon a rock.¶

George Mason said: *"As to the States being in possession of the right to import, that was the case with many other rights now, properly, to be given up.* [Read: *up."*] *He held it essential, in every point of view, that the General Government should have power to prevent the increase of Slavery."* [Read: *Slavery.*] The Convention, practically, exercised the power itself; and Slavery acquiesced. At once, it entered upon its control in the premises by fixing the term of the license, and Slavery accepted the limitation. If the States had not "given up" the right, what need was there of a license at all?¶

There can be no question as to what the power was that the Convention designed to reserve to the General Government. The circumstance that means inadequate to the end proposed were relied on, may prove something against the judgment or sagacity of the Convention, but nothing whatever against its intent or the power it designed to grant. The error of the Convention was, however, the common error of the time; it was in supposing, that the suppression of the slave-trade was all that was needed to suppress Slavery altogether. We know better, but few or none, then living, knew it.¶

It really does not appear, that slavehold-**[41]**ing clung to the power, as tenaciously, as slave-trading did. George Mason's "Eastern brethren" were, apparently, more anxious that the "right to import" should remain with the States, than the Southern dele-

were potential enough to hinder the domestic action of the Congress, but not enough so to modify or restrain its public confession of faith. Hence the difference between the faith and the works of that body, of which the Chief Justice would take a mean advantage.¶

Confident in "the general opinion of the men of that day" that Slavery "would be evanescent and pass away," it rested from its labors, not doubting that it had announced principles which, under corresponding agencies, would soon obliterate the incongruity between those principles and the actual condition of a portion of the people of the country.¶

More than one of the Signers has recorded his sorrow that he was obliged to leave to time what he would gladly have done on the instant; not one has had recourse to the infamous alternative imagined by the Chief Justice. Without contending for a very high moral condition of the world at large, it may be affirmed, that at no time has it been low enough to make possible such relations as are implied in the notion of the Chief Justice, that by some general yet tacit understanding, "the distinguished men who framed the Declaration of Independence" were to affirm, in an unusually solemn manner, very noble things without meaning them, and receive "the sympathy of mankind" for thus forswearing themselves.¶

If the Chief Justice of 1856 had inquired of Mr. Taney of 1818 why he could not then "point without a blush" to the same language he was now quoting without that modest embarrassment, he would have discovered that the cause of shame was not that the Signers had spoken falsely, but that their successors, to so great an extent, had acted falsely; that the one had failed to redeem the honor the other had rightfully and solemnly pledged. That it was his own consciousness that the Signers had uttered truths, and that they were contemned by so many of his countrymen, had caused him then to blush for their faithlessness; but now, himself rejecting the same truths, and imputing falsehood to

to "the descendants" of anybody; and if both provisions had absolutely attainted the subjects of them, the posterity of neither would have suffered on account of it. In many ways, a "person held to service or labor in one State, under the laws thereof," might satisfy such liability, to the perfect contentment of the party by whom such service or labor was claimed, and so render the provision nugatory in respect to himself. By what process might the children of such exempt be brought within the scope of it? If neither he, nor the children born to him in that condition, are under ban of this provision, where in the Constitution is there one that separates him or them from the mass of population, who, like them, are also free from it? What distinction, and if any, where and how, does the Constitution make it, between such as "have purchased this freedom with a great price," and those who are "free-born?" and *a fortiori,* what distinction between the posterity of them? are not both "free-born?"

How much the Chief Justice depended upon a false representation of the text and intent of these clauses, is disclosed, by his persistent iteration of the calumny and the variety of uses to which it is put. Except to execute these two provisions, one might think the General Government had but little to do; and, indeed, that there abode in the Constitution, but little energy for any other purpose. The Chief Justice says:

> "The only two provisions which point to them and include them, treat them as property, and make it the duty of the Government to protect it; **[53]**no other power, in relation to this race, is to be found in the Constitution; and as it is a Government of special, delegated powers, no authority beyond these two provisions can be constitutionally exercised."

Some might think the right to be accounted a person and not a chattel, was rather too valuable a one to be despised or ignored by a Chief Justice in the exercise of his function, but nowhere will it be impotent enough not to convict him of falsehood in saying these provisions "treat them as property."

> people of color who were born on that soil, and that they were not, by the Constitution of 1780 of that State, admitted to the condition of citizens, would be received with surprise by the people of that State, who know their own political history. It is true, beyond all controversy, that persons of color, descended from African slaves, were by that Constitution made citizens of the State; and such of them as had the necessary qualifications, have held and exercised the elective franchise as citizens, from that time to the present. (See Con. *v.* Aves, 18 Pick. R.)"

The learned Justice, also shows, that in the Congress of all the States, the citizenship of colored persons in some of the States was recognized, and in virtue of it, their right to general citizenship was confessed and protected. He says:

> "The fourth of the fundamental articles of the Confederation was as follows: 'The free inhabitants of each of these States, paupers, vagabonds, and fugitives from justice excepted, shall be entitled to all the privileges and immunities of free citizens in the several States.'
>
> "The fact that free persons of color were citizens of some of the several States, and the consequence, that this fourth article of the Confederation would have the effect to confer on such persons the privileges and immunities of general citizenship, were not only known to those who framed and adopted those articles, but the evidence is decisive, that the fourth article was intended to have that effect, and that more restricted language, which would have excluded such persons, was deliberately and purposely rejected.
>
> "On the 25th of June, 1778, the Articles of Confederation being under consideration by the Congress, the delegates from South Carolina moved to amend this fourth article, by inserting after the word 'free,' and before the word 'inhabitants' the word 'white,' so that privileges and immunities of general citizenship would be secured only to white persons. Two States voted for the amendment, eight States against it, and the vote of one State was divided. The language of the article stood unchanged, and both by its terms of inclusion, 'free inhabitants,' and the strong implication from its terms of exclusion, 'paupers, vagabonds, and fugitives

[3]MEMORIAL.

EXCEPTING lawyers, who knows or cares about the great case of Perrin *vs*. Blake; yet, in its day, it excited the bench and bar of England to an uncommon degree; and by its relations to all the realty and not a little of the personalty of the kingdom, may be supposed to have interested nearly the entire ownership of the country. Only two years later, the same court, that of King's Bench, decided another case, involving nothing but the personal liberty of one of the humblest of a degraded race, a negro called Somerset, and alleged to be a slave; yet now, after the lapse of more than ninety years, it would be hard to find, either in England or this country, a tolerably well informed person of any calling who does not know something of this case—more, perhaps, of Somerset, the negro, than of the "Proud Duke" himself.

Perhaps there is nothing that ought to surprise in the circumstance, that a decision in so distant a jurisdiction, affecting only property within it, possesses no general interest among us; but it is very evident that a judgment, by the same tribunal, touching the personal rights of one of the most obscure and powerless of human beings, is of popular and abiding importance both here and there. The argument of Mr. Hargrave, the decision of Mansfield, in the one case, are now read with avidity by multitudes, not one of whom could be enticed to con a page of argument or judgment in the other. The gravest decisions, concerning property merely, are remitted to **[4]**the study of the relatively few whose vocation it is to wage and decide the legal controversies of society. The truth would seem to be, certainly so far as the Anglo-Saxon race is concerned, that public feeling can be extensively and permanently interested only by adjudications bearing upon the personal rights of man.

It is with judges as with their judgments. None are so conspicuously or positively placed in the estimation of mankind; neither the fame nor the infamy of any is so wide-spread or enduring as of those who, in the mercy or the wrath of God, have been vouchsafed opportunity to deny and abrogate, or to declare and maintain by the authority of their office, the rights and privileges of their fellow-creatures. The serenity of the respect, or reverence rather, felt by mankind toward judges who have been bold and just in such relations, is in strong contrast with the activity and energy of the disgust and hatred with which those of the contrary character are regarded.¶

The honorable fame of Sir Matthew Hale has neither the proportions nor the intensity of the infamy of Jeffreys; and it may be doubted whether it will prove as lasting. To forget Jeffreys, the Patriotism and the Protestantism of the world must first put away the memory of their best remembered and most venerated martyrs and confessors. Little as the one is likely to forget Baxter or the other Sydney, as little is Humanity likely to forget either, or Alice Lisle and other victims of the Bloody Assizes.

The vehement antipathy of cultivated man to injustice and cruelty, not only sharpens these judgments in the case of judicial malefactors, but when communities are well instructed, it leads to such promptness in enforcing, as well as in forming them, that not unfrequently, the culprit, who solaced himself with the hope, that, at the worst, his memory, and not himself, would be arraigned, has been overtaken by punishment before his body reached the refuge of the grave.¶

History records but few examples so monitory and illustrative of the certainty and swiftness with which popular justice sometimes avenges wrong of this sort, as that of the late Chief Justice of the United States.

---

[5]For more than twenty years, at every term of the court, the late Chief Justice had pronounced its decisions and delivered his own opinions, without causing much shock to the public sensibilities or special concentration of public attention to any one of them, though many were important. It had come to be felt that the seat vacated by Marshall, was occupied indeed but not filled; and it was notorious that other seats on the bench of that Court had been bestowed upon some without learning or ability enough to entitle them to appear at its Bar, to reward partisan services as questionable in character as those by which he had obtained his own.¶

The court, as then constituted, was less an object of hope than of apprehension to the people; and the public disappointment that so little good was dispensed by it, was soothed by the reflection, that if but little had been bestowed perhaps much had been escaped.

Then the Chief Justice delivered an opinion, which he designed, by the concurrence of obsequious brethren, to foist upon the country as a decision of the court. The case happened to be of the class in which all mankind persist in entering their appearance; and although the scheme failed, and thus saved the court, so manifest was the intent and purpose of the Chief Justice, that the discomfiture brought no mitigation of the responsibility to which he was held.¶

From that hour it ceased to be remembered that he had ever made any other decision; nor so long as the remembrance of these times may endure will it be forgotten that he made that one. He held the scales of justice so foully in the one case, that it was nothing that he might have held them fairly in many. Such right as he had done was to property—the wrong to humanity. Seven more years of terms, judgments and opinions, were granted to the Chief Justice, but they availed not to divert the eyes of men from the one decision; and he closed a life of eighty-seven years, and a judicial career of seven and twenty, leaving but one memory behind him.

Zeal in behalf of an unnatural and demoralizing institution, one as much opposed to the Constitution of the country as to its moral sense, led him, in an evil hour to undertake to legalize and hallow it, and that, too, by extra-judicial means. When he volunteered this service he was eighty years old, and he per-**[6]**formed it in contempt of settled rules of law and the practice of his own court.¶

Mr. Justice Curtis, in his opinion in the case, says:

> "Having first decided that they were bound to consider the sufficiency of the plea to the jurisdiction of the Circuit Court, and having decided that this plea showed that the Circuit Court had not jurisdiction, and consequently that this is a case to which the judicial power of the United States does not extend, they have gone on to examine the merits of the case as they appeared on the trial before the court and jury, on the issues joined on the pleas in bar, and so have reached the question of the power of Congress to pass the act of 1820. On so grave a subject as this, I feel obliged to say that, in my opinion, such an exertion of judicial power transcends the limits of the authority of the court, as described by its repeated decisions, and, as I understand, acknowledged in this opinion of the majority of the court."

The Chief Justice took nothing that he proposed by the usurpation; and only succeeded in welding to his own, the name of his intended victim and the memory of the injustice and cruelty he designed toward him and four millions of his race, then in being, and their endless posterity. The annals of slavery furnish no such instance of patient and faithful following as Dred Scott has, and will forever exhibit, in his shadow-like attendance upon the name and memory of Roger B. Taney.

Roger Brooke Taney was born in Calvert County, Maryland, March 17th, 1777, and died, in Washington, October 12th, 1864. He was educated at Dickinson College, Pennsylvania; studied law and was admitted to practice, in 1799, at Annapolis, in his native State. There can be no doubt that he attained high professional standing at the local bar. He achieved some political distinction also; for he was early elected to the Legislature, and, in 1816, was a State Senator. In 1823, he quit the provinces for the capital, and, after a residence of four years in Baltimore, was appointed Attorney-General of Maryland.

Originally a Federalist, like Buchanan and others of certain proclivities, he came to sympathize, politically, with the party which promised to be best able to reward service; and shrewdly commended himself to its rising man, General Jackson, by vehement applause of his Bank policy. He received the first installment of gratitude from the warm-hearted President Jackson, in 1831, in the form of the Attorney-Generalship of the United States. His opinion in the matter of Gwinn's appointment is quite enough to show to what extent he regarded the **[7]**people of the United States as his clients, and to what extent his patron. It was a natural sequence of events that, in 1833, when the then Secretary of the Treasury, William J. Duane, proved impracticable in the affair of removing the public deposits from the Bank of the United States, the President replaced such a Secretary by Mr. Taney, whom he knew to be incapable of exhibiting even a caricature of personal or political independence. Mr. Taney was obviously the man for the hour. The Senate, however, declined to reward such complaisance by confirming his nomination.¶

It was an idiosyncrasy of General Jackson to hate the Supreme Court, and he never missed an opportunity to do it an injury; so, in 1835, when the resignation of Judge Duvall created a vacancy on its bench, he nominated his "pliant friend," Taney, for the place. The Senate had not declined sufficiently to permit the consummation of this purpose either, and again Mr. Taney encountered its rejection of his nomination. But, by the time of its session in March, 1836, important changes had occurred in the composition of the body, and by a mournful coincidence, as it was then thought, the providence of God had opened the most vital joint in the armor of the Supreme Court. Its just, firm and learned chief, John Marshall, was dead. The irritated President, at once, nominated Roger B. Taney for the high place; and the majority of the Senate, void of the instincts necessary to apprehend the unfitness of the act, confirmed his nomination.¶

A long series of opinions, too trite even to be quoted and too dull to be read, which would not confer distinction upon a judge of the most inferior judicatory in the land, and the Dred Scott decision, which would disgrace any man or jurist in Christendom, are an all-sufficient justification of the minority of the Senate, which steadily refused to consent to the substitution, in so lofty and important a position, of suppleness for firmness, of obsequiousness for independence, of mediocrity in all things for greatness in all things.¶

On the other hand, such consequences of the action of that majority are before us, that, without at all relieving its moral aspect, make it questionable, whether the human race has not profited more by its subserviency, than if it, **[8]**too, had refused consent to this nomination? Who has done so much, as its appointee, to hasten the downfall of Slavery?

Mr. Taney passed his whole life in the valley and shadow of Slavery. Born and reared in the midst of servile institutions, his opinions of their worth and character escaped modification by the clamor of what men called uninformed revilers of the system, or the testimony of "prejudiced witnesses," as the phrase ran. Whatever his estimate of the moral, social and economical tendencies of the institution, it was founded, entirely, on his personal obser-

his opinions on that subject whenever he pleases. It is a subject of national concern, and may at all times be freely discussed. Mr. Gruber did quote the language of our great act of national independence, and insisted on the principles contained in that venerated instrument. He did rebuke those masters, who, in the exercise of power, are deaf to the calls of humanity, and he warned them of the evils they might bring upon themselves. He did speak with abhorrence of those reptiles who live by trading in human flesh, and enrich themselves by tearing the husband from the wife, the infant from the bosom of the mother; and this, I am instructed, was the head and front of his offending.¶

"Shall I content myself by saying he had a right to say this? that there is no law to punish him? So far is he from being the object of punishment in any form of proceeding, that we are prepared to maintain the same principles, and to use, if necessary, the same language here, in the temple of justice, and in the presence of those who are the ministers of the law.

"A hard necessity, indeed, compels us to endure the evils of Slavery for a time. It was imposed upon us by another nation while yet we were in a state of colonial vassalage. It cannot be easily or suddenly removed. Yet, while it continues, it is a blot on our national character, and every real lover of Freedom confidently hopes that it will be effectually, though it must be gradually, wiped away, and earnestly looks for the means by which this necessary object may be attained. And, until it shall be accomplished, until the time come when we can point without a blush to the language held in the Declaration of Independence, every friend of humanity will seek to lighten the galling chain of Slavery, and better, to the utmost of his power, the wretched condition of the slave."

[10]It appears to have been divinely ordered that original impulses, neither of revealed religion, natural justice nor philanthropy, should be suffered to destroy American Slavery, but that it shall invite or provoke its own doom by foolish truculence toward them all. In this instance, the obnoxious sermon had been preached at a camp-meeting, in the county of Washington, and there, probably, its force would have been spent. Slavery was not wise enough to let it alone; and by the malice of its scourged devotees, the doctrines so much dreaded came to be proclaimed by a more potential voice, in the county of Frederick, "in the temple of justice and in the presence of those who are the ministers of the law," in a pioneer case, the decision of which would of necessity become a precedent.¶

It is not easy to determine the degree in which the future of Slavery in Maryland was shaped by this timely rescue, by Mr. Taney, of "the control of future discussions on this great and important question," from "passion, prejudice and avarice;" by his unqualified claim that "any man has the right to publish his opinions on that subject whenever he pleases;" by his scathing denunciation of "those reptiles who live by trading in human flesh;" by his declaration that the system is a "blot on our national character," yet so certain to be "effectually," if "gradually," "wiped away," that the only debateable point in regard to its extinction was that of time; by the respect he exhibited toward the "language of our great act of national independence," and insisting "on the principles contained in that venerated instrument."¶

If to the effect of these reinforcements of the cause of Freedom be added the force of moral and political resistance to that of its adversary, evoked by the Dred Scott decision, it will be found difficult to name another who has done so much as Mr. Taney to bring Slavery to its end in Maryland. Thousands served Freedom with more constancy than he, not one harmed Slavery so much.¶

A coincidence which emphasized his death, has been much remarked upon. The final hour came to Slavery and himself simultaneously. His dying finger could "point without a blush to the language held in the Declaration of Independence;" for the same twelfth day of October that re-**[11]**lieved Maryland from Slavery, delivered both Maryland and the world from Roger B. Taney.

As if to make the abyss seem deeper, into which, as Chief Justice be voluntarily cast himself, Mr. Taney, the advocate, ascended to a loftier pinnacle than his merely professional obligations required. His strict professional duty was discharged when he had claimed and obtained for his client all the rights secured to him by the laws of the jurisdiction, and there he might have rested. But, touched by the humanity and patriotism of Gruber, he went farther, and asserted for himself and for all men, as well as for his client, rights which the law neither gave nor could take away, rights underived and inalienable by statute, founding their claim to be respected by courts as well as men, upon what has latterly been a rare recourse for any such purpose, their recognition and reaffirmance by "our great act of national independence."¶

Except Fourth of July orators, who speaks now of the Declaration of Independence? Do they speak of it on any other day? Yet, Mr. Taney insisted "on the principles contained in that venerated instrument," on a day purely secular, on an occasion not festive.

"That venerated instrument," reverenced by Mr. Taney in this exemplary manner, has been held so sacred in this land that men of parts and position have forfeited respect while living, and dead are remembered with disgust, because they prostituted fine powers to sneering at its sublime truths and impeaching its earnestness. If the American people could, now, so sink, that what has hitherto been exceptional and individual might be held to be general and popular, and by equal derision of the principles of the Declaration earn national infamy as profound, it is entirely probable that its "glittering generalities" would still provoke respect from the rest of mankind, and even the Fourth of July might become the festival of "foreign nations and the next age."

Notwithstanding the popular respect vouchsafed to the Declaration by its title, the consciousness that it is, and must forever be, a valid, subsisting obligation upon the American people, seems limited among us to a degree that hardly consists with the sincerity of so general professions of respect for its **[12]**principles. It may be that from the eyes of most it is hidden by the Constitution, or rather that [it] is superseded or rendered nugatory by it; which may be the case to some extent, in an exceedingly narrow and technical sense. Whatever the cause, the fact remains, that it has come to be regarded by too many as something entirely respectable but obsolete; or at the most, as a purely domestic or national affair with which no people but our own ever had any concern whatever. It must lie reverenced because of the authorship of it, and of the associations that cluster around its adoption; but, in respect to power and authority, as having outlived both. It must he admired but need not be obeyed.¶

An idea more charged with mischief has never obtained currency among the people. It is full of warning to the honest and thoughtful that one so false in fact, in morals and in equity, has received any hospitality at all. So long as our present independence may endure, every citizen will be bound in morals and in honor, to maintain the doctrines and policy of the Declaration, and to give them effect, on every occasion and by every means, not forbidden by the Constitution and laws passed in pursuance thereof.

That Declaration is not, nor never was in any sense, a matter between the States, united or otherwise, nor the people of the States and the Continental Congress. The instrument is in nature, if not in form, a treaty or compact, the parties to which are named therein, and the Congress of '76 is not one of them. That was a representative body—nothing more, and certainly, nothing less. It was careful to imbed in the text of the instrument itself, a notice to all mankind, that it declared and covenanted not for itself, nor yet for states or colonies, but "in the name and by the authority of the good people of these colonies," and "all the people said Amen."¶

The Declaration is a registry of the birth, not of colonies

separate and sovereign, nor of states separate and sovereign, but of the people of the United States, "in the name and by the authority" of whom alone, the colonies were transformed from separate into United States. If the record stood without any correlative support whatever, it would be ample to discredit the pretense, that a separate, selfish independence was even so much as named by **[13]**any one of the old Thirteen, much less acquired by one of them. Not a state in the Union, Massachusetts as little as South Carolina, ever claimed, declared or acquired any independence whatever, except the joint one, first declared and then conquered "in the name and by the authority of the good people of these colonies." It has never been divided nor is it susceptible of division; and this day the people of South Carolina have an undivided and indivisible interest in the independence of Massachusetts and of every other State in the Union. The people of the United States, "one and indivisible," are the parties of the first part to that momentous Declaration, and they are the sole proprietors of the independence declared thereby.

A very natural counterparty to the people, whose first profession was "a decent respect for the opinions of mankind," is the one they named with such distinctness as defies cavil—"a candid world." It was the American people who called upon God to witness their covenant—it was "a candid world" that heard, believed, and trusted.

The right of that Congress to represent "the good people of these colonies" was never denied by the people represented. Who can acquire a right to challenge it now? By that Congress, this Nation covenanted with God and "a candid world" to shed the blood of the Revolution for the causes and purposes set forth in its Declaration, and for no others. When the patriots of that body pledged "lives, fortunes, and sacred honor," to the support of the principles and purposes announced in the Declaration and suscribed it with their names, every individual of the nation was as solemnly bound to the same things as John Hancock himself. And so is every citizen now. What authority can absolve one of them?

Who can absolve himself?

"A candid world" seems to have been propitiated by the deference to its opinions exhibited by the American people, and to have regarded with favor even, the objects to which it was declared the force of the Revolution would be applied. Except, of course, the power whose jurisdiction was to be ousted, not one in all Europe proved unfriendly; several contributed substantial "aid and comfort," and the least favor received from **[14]**any was forbearance.¶

But was that the least? Our appreciation of the worth of what the nation received from "a candid world," on the score of its avowed intentions, ought to be sharpened not a little, by contrasting what we have received, mainly, from the same quarter, during our present struggle to preserve the independence acquired by the Revolution. If the rebellious and the loyal can recall their emotions, when the one hoped and the other dreaded European intervention in aid of the Slaveholders' Rebellion, both will be aided in estimating the real value of forbearance to the one side and the loss of it to the other. Contrast the France of to-day and the France of the Revolution. Now she harbors Semmes and builds privateers to harm us; then she fitted out fleets and sent Rochambeaus to help us. The fact is undeniable that, upon the faith of our Declaration, France contributed money, ships, and men, Holland loaned us money, and other nations exercised a comity, of such value, that, upon the whole, it may be affirmed, that, without the moral and material aid furnished by the party of the second part under the Declaration, "a candid world," no such independence would have existed as we are this day fighting to maintain.

It may be stated as a proposition, that the American people never had, nor can they acquire, the right to use an independence thus obtained, for purposes inconsistent with the solemn pledges made in their Declaration, upon the faith of which they received aid from some, forbearance from others, and success from God.

even the spirit, of that compact, has been followed by consequences so unequivocal in character, and so prompt in point of time, that it is impossible not to see that the one was the direct result of the other. How they illustrate and enforce the utterances of George Mason in the Constitutional Convention: "As nations cannot be rewarded or punished in the next world, they must be in this. By an inevitable chain of causes and effects, Providence punishes national sins by national calamities."

The immediate use to which the people put their newly asserted independence, was one entirely subversive of the main object of the Declaration. That, object was to create a Free People; to add another to the family of Nations; the use was **[16]**to establish a confederation of independent States. The difference between the two things ought to be palpable to us, seeing that the Declaration contemplated the precise *status* the United States are now striving to maintain; while the thing done is precisely that which the Slaveholders' Rebellion is trying to re-establish, with certain aggravations. The parties of the first part, the People of the United States, came not upon the stage. Instead of a national constitution, to shield public and private rights, and provide for uniformity in the administration of the government, there was unfurled to the eyes of the world, "Articles of Confederation and Perpetual Union between" thirteen distinct and independent sovereignties! Another robust and well-proportioned nation would have been welcomed by the rest; but thirteen abortions, and illegitimate at that, without members or senses to serve their own needs or discharge international duties, was not an addition calculated to bring credit or advantage to the family. It was not "the entertainment to which they had been invited," and signally was the disappointment avenged. This was our first flagrant departure from the principles and policy of the Declaration.

Remembering the vast hoard of practical sense, as well as of patriotism, possessed, beyond all question, by the public men of that day, it is amazing that such a system as that of the Confederation ever obtained a footing. But for Professor Tayler Lewis' remarkable production, entitled “A Photograph from the Ruins of Greece,” it might be supposed human folly had never before gone to such a length; but if with that experience and the learned Professor's exposition of it, any such scheme shall again be even entertained, it will be much more surprising. Its Congress had power to contract debts and pledge the public faith for the payment of them; but it was without resources wherewith to pay them. It could merely ascertain the sums of money necessary to be raised, and apportion to each State its quota. It is notorious, however, that not even the dangers of the existing war were enough to terrify the States into respect for the recommendations of its Congress in regard to money; though subjugation by the common enemy seemed a present consequence of the want of it. It was the opinion of discreet men **[17]**that but for the loans made in France and Holland, the revolution would not have gone beyond rebellion. And after the peace, Congress was not able to extract money enough from the States to pay the interest on the debt of the Revolution. It was without power to levy a tax or collect a duty for the public service—that right belonged to the States.¶

Motley, the historian, describing this epoch, says: “Seventy years ago we were a helpless league of bankrupt and lawless petty sovereignties. We had a currency so degraded that a leg of mutton was cheap at a thousand dollars. The national debt, incurred in the war of independence, had hardly a nominal value, and was considered worthless. The absence of law, order, and security for life and property, was as absolute as could well be conceived in a civilized land. Debts could not be collected, courts could enforce no decrees, insurrections could not be suppressed. The army of the Confederation numbered eighty men.” (Letter to the *London Times*). It was feeble enough to be defied at home, but abroad, the Confederation was simply despised. No considerable foreign power could be enticed into treaty relations with it. Great Britain declined to surrender the Western military posts, provided for in the treaty of peace, on the ground that some of the sovereignties had, by legislation, obstructed the collection of British debts.

This shameful condition lasted ten years, four of them free from the impediments of public war, before enough unanimity of action was compelled, on the part of the sovereignties, to permit a remedy. Thus, the same people who had shown themselves vigorous enough to contend for seven years with the most powerful nation on earth, for their own nationality, was so prostrated by that political anaesthetic State Rights, that not until 1787 did the Nation, as such, lift its head.¶

It made good use, however, of its recovered consciousness. By the ratification of the people of the several States, in Conventions called for the special purpose, and not by the ordinary machinery of their State governments, our present Constitution, and the Laws "made in pursuance thereof," became "the supreme law of the land;"—anything in the "Constitution or laws of any State to the contrary notwithstanding."

[18]"The effects of the new Constitution," says Motley, "were almost magical. Order sprang out of chaos; law resumed its reign; debts were collected; life and property became secure; the national debt was funded and ultimately paid, principal and interest, to the utmost farthing; the articles of the treaty of peace were fulfilled; and Great Britain, having an organized and united state to deal with, entered into a treaty of commerce and amity with us—the first and the best ever negotiated between the two nations. Not the least noble of its articles (the 21st) provided that the acceptance by the citizens or subjects of either country of foreign letters of marque should be treated and *punished as piracy.* Unfortunately, that article and several others were limited to twelve years, and were not subsequently renewed. The debts due to British subjects were collected, and the British government at last surrendered the forts on our soil." (*Letter to the London Times.*)

The inhering nature of the allegiance due to "the principles contained in that venerated instrument," the Declaration, from every member of the commonwealth of which it is the charter, has been asserted; and the consequent absence of all right on their part to make constitutions or establish institutions opposed to its liberal spirit, has been insisted on. The framers of the Constitution certainly acted in conformity with such views of duty and of privilege.¶

The harmony between the political objects specified in the preamble to their Constitution and the rights claimed by the Continental Congress in their Declaration, is quite too perfect to have been accidental; and neither in their words or works does anything appear inconsistent with the idea that they were conscious of the incapacity alleged. They confessed, fortified, adjusted and applied the pre-existing organic obligation in a manner, to a degree and under sanctions, not practicable under the Declaration. The Apostles' Creed is of authority in many churches, but it does not establish an ecclesiastical polity in one of them; and so the Declaration, although it prescribed, for want of certain faculties, could not administer its own prescriptions. Systems of discipline and administration are supplementary arrangements, but always loyal and subordinate to the confession of faith designed to be utilized. The **[19]**Constitution provided executive, legislative, and judicial instrumentalities, and for what purposes? The Constitution answers this question best. Its intent is to be found in its own preamble. It is expressed nowhere else—there it is set forth in singularly plain terms.¶

If among many provisions devised to give effect to that intent, a few should prove not well calculated for the purpose, it would argue nothing against the intent, but would simply illustrate a familiar infirmity of human wisdom—a failure to adapt means to ends wisely. If one gives a promissory note conditioned *not* to pay, the maker is held liable to pay in our jurisprudence, because such is the universal intent of that species of obligation; and the negation implies but error or fraud on the part of the maker, in neither of which will the law protect him. Intent controls the text—not the text the intent.¶

If the Constitution had not declared its own intent, it might be inferred; but having expressed it, inference is altogether improper and superfluous. The intent of the Constitution and the doctrines of the Declaration harmonize strictly, so far as the Constitution goes. Indeed the Constitution is but the Declaration in action.

To citizens like the Framers and Mr. Taney of 1818, the Declaration stands as the Gospel does to the Christian—the rule of faith; the guide of counsel; the model for imitation; the acme of attainment. The truth is, the Federal Constitution was made in the spirit and in fulfillment of the Declaration, which was impotent to execute though competent to ordain, and by its light it ought to be construed. If ingenious disloyalty attempts its own justification, by alleging some incongruity between the letter of some directory provision of the one and the grandly just and simple inculcations of the other, let none be moved by the effort. The premises will be found to be false or the argument sophistical.¶

The Constitution, like the Declaration, was the result of necessity as well as choice. The circumstances of the country compelled it. The disastrous aberration in the case of the Confederacy had demonstrated that "the path of duty, of honor and of safety," led to the doctrines and policy of our *Magna Charta;* and in that path the Framers trod. It was no purpose of theirs to remedy **[20]**deviations from the principles to which the Nation was bound, and for abandonment of which it was then suffering, by still wider and more confirmed departures. They were too wise and too honest for that. The country cried to them for bread—they gave it not a stone. They were too humane for that. The country had a confederation and demanded "a more perfect union;" especially they did not respond by making provision for another confederation, but by making another impossible.

Until actual conflict between, not the letter of some

phrase, but the indisputable intent of the Constitution and "our great act of national independence" is positively established, the latter will remain to the end, as it was at the beginning, of imperial obligation on every citizen of the republic. If any such conflict could be shown, there can be no question that the claims of the Constitution would be paramount in the premises.¶

Yet, the Framers were provident enough to take care that no such contingency should operate as a license to injustice or impolicy in perpetuity. Hence, the Constitution provides for its own amendment to any extent for which experience or progress may develop a necessity. The preamble, which embodies the intent, is not amendable indeed, but the provisions executory of that intent are indefinitely so. They may be made efficient to whatever degree the wisdom of the country shall be able to make them.¶

To alter the Constitution in its objects and purposes would be simply to abolish it, and would not in any sense be an exercise of the right to amend. Beside, the rights covered by the purposes declared in the preamble are not conferred by the Constitution. They were extant and hoary with age before the Constitution was made, or the Declaration either. Neither creates them—both recognize and reassure them—the rights themselves—derived from God, are inalienable in living man, who can divest neither himself nor his posterity of them by any compact or agreement even if he calls it a constitution. Man's true relation to the vast fund of human rights is that of beneficiary—not of benefactor, as some seem to think. The use is his—the fund is not his. The right to enjoy begins at the cradle, and ends at the **[21]**grave of every man born into the world. No man has been nor can be born to the slightest right to appropriate, to squander or to alienate, the trust fund. Every human being is a *cestui que trust* and nothing less—no child of Adam, of right, is or can be more—nor, can one *cestui que trust* rob another without incurring the guilt of that crime.

The Declaration asserted the natural right of all men, everywhere, among other things, to "life, liberty, and the pursuit of happiness;" and further, "that to secure these rights, govern-

tained in "our great act of national independence," for the security and maintenance of which alone the Constitution itself was established.

With our experience of the embarrassments arising from the presence of Slavery in the country, it is not hard to understand that the framers had severe trials in dealing with it. It was more diffused then than now. It was an existing condition at the time in every State but Massachusetts. While it refused to submit itself, wholly and instantly, to the authority of the Convention, it pertinaciously forced its claims upon it to be recognized and protected by the coming Constitution.¶

The framers did deal with it, however, and in this connection it should always be borne in mind, that those who dealt with it were themselves slaveholders, or represented slaveholding communities, with the exception only of those from Massachusetts. It was essentially an adjudication by slavery itself, awakened to consciousness of its own moral, social, and economical tendencies, concerning itself. Neither William Lloyd Garrison nor Wendell Phillips were there. None were so active or potential in that Convention as slaveholders.¶

It may be said, with entire truth, that Slavery made the Constitution, and through shame excluded itself from its purview. Perhaps remorse was not without its share in extorting from Slavery that quit claim to every part and parcel of the domain of Liberty.¶

In the face of this action on the part of Slavery itself, men, born and nurtured under free institutions, and who owe the consideration that makes their errors dangerous to the absence of that spirit of caste by which Slavery lives and moves, are not ashamed to say: "Our Fathers found it impossible to form a Union, without recognizing and protecting slavery." "Our Fathers" refused to do either the one or the other, though urgently importuned to do both; for Slavery was not without attorneys and advocates then as well as now. Seeing so much was demanded, the Framers **[23]**are entitled to gratitude for not having done more, rather than censure for doing what they did.

The provision for reclaiming fugitives from "service or labor," was, unquestionably, "a sop to Cerberus;" and the guilt of adopting it attaches to the Framers. But their sin becomes "white as wool," contrasted with ours, in our gratuitous and ceaseless offering of human sacrifices to that dirty dog. No fair or sensible construction of the provision constrained us to it.

In point of fact, the Convention had been nigh to doing much worse. A proposition to reckon the value of three-fifths of the slaves in estimating taxes, and making taxation the basis of representation, was once agreed to in committee—a positive recognition of "property in man." But there were in the body, men, from whose garments the dust of the battle fields of the Revolution had scarcely been brushed; others to whom the solemn hour when they affixed their names to the Declaration was still fresh, and all remembered the fraternal relations that had been enforced among the people by the common perils of the war of Independence. Was it for this we fought from Lexington to Yorktown? What will be the judgment of "a candid world" upon acts like this? were questions that doubtless presented themselves to such defenders of human rights and exemplars of personal honor. The action of the Convention, at all events, answered such questions most distinctly.

It is the practice of that burdensome and discontented class of our people, who are barren of patriotism, because they are without morals or intelligence enough to beget that virtue, to charge upon such Christian ministers as felt it their duty to denounce the sins that confronted them, rather than the short-comings of the mummies in the Egyptian catacombs, and the abolitionists proper, who, until the war broke out, were a mere handful, the production of the present civil war, by their speaking ill of

Slavery, and counseling the rapine of "its rights under the Constitution."¶

This preposterous accusation has been made so persistently by some who, from their position and associations, enjoyed the imputation of being truthful and intelligent, that even well-intentioned ignorance has been led to doubt whether there might not have been some day in the country, **[24]**when the institution was thought to be "just, benign, beneficent," and that it really had been once "endowed with certain inalienable rights" to appropriate to its own use, the "life, liberty, and property," of indefinite millions of the human race.¶

Now, the sun never shone upon any such day. Slavery never had any such rights. It is scarcely so odious now as it was in 1787. No recent denunciations of it can be shown, that equal in power and intensity those showered upon it by its proprietors and guardians in the Constitutional Convention. As for "its rights under the Constitution," let us see what they were.

It has been stated that once Slavery received recognition by the Convention. The acquaintance never ripened into intimacy. The results of reflection were disclosed very soon after in debates. Mr. Madison thought "it wrong to admit in the Constitution the idea that there could be property in man.["] (Madison Papers, III., 1429.) The institution was denounced generally, even by such as were inclined to tolerate it on grounds of interest, and defended by none, it is believed, on its merits. The Convention concurred in sentiment with Mr. Madison, and an alteration in the phraseology of a clause of the Constitution was subsequently made to avoid an implication unfavorable to that view. This was the character of the ultimate action of the Convention. How its conclusiveness is increased by the fact, that its final action was subversive of its first! The correction of an error, the reversal of a decision, imply thought and deliberation at all times; but on this occasion, recalling the nature of the question, the gravity of the consequences threatened, and of the results desired, there is no escape from the conclusion, that the deliberate, well-considered purpose of the Framers, proved also by the text of the Constitution itself, was not to recognize the *status* of slavery at all, nor protect one of its alleged rights; but on the contrary to exclude, totally and forever, from the Constitution, its text and intent, "the idea that there could be property in man."

That a provision of the Constitution, although including free white persons in its scope, still was intended to operate among the very class whose existence was ignored, is admitted; and at first, it might seem that good faith had been violated in **[25]**some quarter. But Slavery understood the matter perfectly, and made no imputation of the kind at the time; it hardly becomes its attorneys to make it now.¶

It is not pleasant to confess that the arrangement then made between Freedom and Slavery may be described by the word "compromise." The Convention was a sort of Humane Society engaged in restoring to life and power the American People, who had been nearly suffocated by the fumes of State Rights. Slavery, which never had, and never can have, any other attitude than to stand with its own feet upon the neck of a slave, while it is itself supported by the energy and strength derived by some other power from more liberal institutions, by instinct demanded the support and protection of the resuscitated nation. "Our Fathers" were virtuous enough to refuse this to Slavery, as such; but not virtuous enough, or perhaps not strong enough, to withhold it altogether from Slavery disguised in the livery of manhood. The most they could be brought to do, in the interest of Slavery, even under this aspect, was to take limited cognizance of its serfs, upon condition that always they should be deemed and taken to be "persons"—never otherwise; in the interest of Freedom, however, no limit or impediment to their enfranchisement was set.

The controlling reason for this is neither doubtful nor obscure. It was claimed to be a State institution, and not in anywise subject to any general jurisdiction. The scandal as well as the profit belonged wholly to the State. No State had ever been, and thenceforth could never be, recognized by any other State or Nation on earth. On the other hand, the United States were to be known, and hold relations with all the world. It was determined that citizens of the United States, as such, should appear innocent of all complicity in the existence or continuance of Slavery. A citizen of Georgia might own a human chattel, if Georgia pleased, for no one knew him; but a citizen of the United States could possess no such thing, for all mankind would recognize him, and he had a character to maintain. The Federal Constitution, to be known and read of all men, included no such thing within its jurisdiction. Every subject was *a person;* and while the personality [personalty] of some was assumed, **[26]**that of the class in question was positively stated, and the equal rights of all persons, under the Constitution, were solemnly guaranteed.

The position of the Convention in reference to the general subject, and the extent of such jurisdiction as it possessed, cannot, perhaps, be better expressed than in Elbridge Gerry's statement of it: that it "had nothing to do with the conduct of the States as to slaves, but ought to be careful not to give any sanction to it." (Madison Papers, III., 1394.) It was without authority to control "the conduct of the States as to slaves," and therefore did not undertake to do it; its right and duty were "to be careful not to give any sanction to it"—this it was.

The action of the Convention sheds a steady light upon its intentions with regard to the general subject; and in respect to the provision already referred to, it almost reveals the processes of reasoning by which it was modified from time to time. As offered originally, it assumed that the fugitive in question was *legally* held. Mr. Madison says: "'legally' was struck out, and the words 'under the laws thereof' inserted after the word 'State,' in compliance with the wish of some who thought the term legal equivocal, and favoring the idea that Slavery was legal in a moral view." (Madison Papers, III., 1589.) The Convention, *"unanimously"* struck out the word "servitude," and inserted "service," on motion of Edmund Randolph, of Virginia, "the former being thought to express the condition of *slaves,* and the latter the obligations of *free* persons." (Madison Papers, III., 1569.) The provision came to be finally in these words: "No person held to service or labor in one State, under the laws thereof, escaping into another, shall, in consequence of any law or regulation therein, be discharged from such service or labor; but shall be delivered up on claim of the party to whom such service or labor may be due." (U. S. Con., Art. IV., Sec. 2.)

If there be one thing, morally, legally and equitably, improper to be done by virtue of this provision, it is the precise thing that has so often been done in its name. Great care was taken that Slavery might never have a day in any Federal court. **[27]**The minutes of the Convention and the text of the Constitution concur in testifying that not any, even the slightest, recognition was intended by the one nor is permitted by the other; yet Federal officials, acting under Federal laws, have surrendered slaves to alleged owners whenever requested, not forbearing to sacrifice the lives of citizens by the military arm of the government when necessary to the accomplishment of their purpose; every such alleged slave being, at the time, "a person," by the express designation of the Constitution, and entitled to its and their protection.¶

There has not been an hour since the adoption of the Constitution, in which any Federal officer has had a right to apprehend, or any Federal judicatory to adjudge, a slave, fugitive or otherwise. Except as *a person,* no slave can be subject to any Federal jurisdiction whatever, civil or criminal, and every one of those adjudications is a usurpation and outrage incapable of justification of any sort.¶

A recognition of a *quasi* relation of debtor and creditor, not an uncommon one among men, was the utmost designed or granted in the premises. The saddest feature is the character of the debt, except, perhaps, the remedy; but debt it is after all. For many a day subsequent to that, the law gave to creditors a remedy against the bodies of their debtors; and it may have seemed

Congress of the nation, its judicial and ministerial officers, are all involved in "the deep damnation of the taking off" of guiltless men, women and children, ostensibly in virtue of, but clearly in contempt of, this unhappy clause.

The Convention, prone by familiarity and antecedent as well as present interests and associations, to judge Slavery leniently, but by the same means eminently qualified to judge it righteously, excluded from the vocabulary of the Constitution the term, and from its contemplation the idea of a slave. A rapidly degenerating but active and enterprising class of the people well nigh succeeded in interpolating both. The word fell upon the ear by the fireside and on the highway, in the forum and from the pulpit, and finally, in the halls of legislation and in the courts of justice.¶

With the word came the idea, and soon the public conscience became hardened as the public ear. Federal marshals, and even independent kidnappers, apprehended fugitive slaves, and Federal Judges and Commissioners delivered persons, not proved to be slaves even, to claimants, not proved to be masters even, and escaped both **[29]**dungeon and gibbet. As if a slave, in any aspect, was a cognizable thing under the Constitution!

The least equivocal, and by far the least defensible feature of the Constitution, is that which licensed the slave trade in fact, but not in terms, for twenty years. The term expired in 1808, and it has long ceased to be a practical question; but the bones which whiten our fields to-day are the harvest of which that, and kindred acts, are the seed. If our first breach of the faith plighted to "a candid world," was, at once, punished by national and political humiliation so profound, that, by a little aid from the imagination, the Genius of the country could be seen crimson with shame and bathed in tears, the door-posts of our dwellings, at least, escaped being stained with blood; but higher crimes against humanity have at length provoked even that terrible vengeance; and now, with oh how little aid from fancy, the country appears like Rachel mourning her children, and "refusing to be comforted because they are not!"

This enormous and conceded wrong was done, avowedly, to secure the ratification of the Constitution by South Carolina and Georgia. John Rutledge, of the former State, roused by the remark of Luther Martin, of Maryland, that "such a feature in the Constitution was inconsistent with the principles of the Revolution and dishonorable to the American character,["] (Madison Papers, III. 1388), substantially admitted the demoralizing and inhuman character of the traffic while, without a blush, he made the toleration of it a *sine qua non.* He said: "Religion and humanity have nothing to do with this question. Interest is the governing principle with nations. The true question at present is, whether the Southern States shall or shall not he parties to the Union. If the Northern States consult their interests, they will not oppose the increase of slaves, which will increase the commodities of which they will become the carriers." (Madison Papers, III. 1389.)¶

This appeal to the lowest of human motives, curiously enough, was responded to by Connecticut. Oliver Ellsworth said: "Let every State import what it pleases. The morality or wisdom of slavery is a consideration belonging to the States. What enriches a part enriches the whole, and the States are the best judges of their **[30]**particular interests." (Madison Papers, III. 1389.) Charles Pinckney, of South Carolina, omitting Rutledge's blasphemous defiance of God and outlawry of man, re-echoed his demand. "South Carolina can never receive the plan if it prohibits the slave trade," said he; and treacherously added: "If the States be left at liberty on this subject, South Carolina may, perhaps, by degrees, do of herself what is wished, as Maryland and Virginia already have done." (Madison Papers, III. 1389.)¶

Again Connecticut spoke. Roger Sherman said: "He [read: said he] disapproved the slave trade, but as the States now possessed the right, and the public good did not require it to be taken away, and as it was expedient to have as few objections as possible to the proposed scheme of government, he would leave the matter as he found it. The abolition of slavery seemed to be going on in the United States, and the good sense of the several States would probably, by degrees, soon complete it." [read: it.] (Madison Papers, III. 1390.)¶

Ellsworth again came to the rescue, and tried to lessen the moral effect of the example set by Maryland and Virginia, by exposing the motive that prompted it. The natural increase of slaves in those States had been so rapid that "it [read: it] was cheaper to raise them there than to import them, while in the sickly rice swamps foreign supplies were necessary. If we stop short with prohibiting their importation, we shall be unjust to South Carolina and Georgia. Let us not intermeddle. As population increases, poor laborers will be so plenty as to render slaves useless. Slavery, in time, will not be a speck in our country;" [read: country;] and human beings were the subject of this debate!¶

Verily, seeing existence was nauseated by such stuff as Touceys and Seymours are made of, there seems a fitness that it was spewed out in the State of Connecticut.

But it is the very refinement of retributive justice that South Carolina gave to the country John C. Calhoun, a man saturated with the spirit of evil and wonderfully equipped for political mischief; yet disguised by such purity and gentleness in private life, that his political aims and purposes, more atrocious and hurtful than those we shudder at in Cataline, only provoked cotemporaries to astonishment or controversy, never to judgment and punishment.¶

And when the time came that **[31]**crime as well as craft was needed to give effect to his counsels, that her yoke-fellow, Georgia, provided a perjured villain like Howell Cobb to sap and mine the national finances, and a bully like Robert Toombs to threaten and intimidate a "Quaker" Senate.¶

There is no power in numbers to express the sum of pecuniary damage to the commonwealth, nor in the imagination to conceive the aggregate of agony and desolation in its households, caused by the rebellion set on foot, mainly, by these two States, for whose sake the American people violated their faith, pledged to "a candid world," and consented to forget God and outrage man for the term of twenty years.

South Carolina was both a clog and a scandal to the United States during the war of Independence. Then, as since, it was a hot-bed of treason to the cause of constitutional liberty and faithless to every obligation of duty or honor. Insolent and cruel to the helpless, servile and fawning to the strong, the State is saved from being an unmitigated curse to the country and the world, only by the accident, that a very few of the most respectable and serviceable men of the Revolution, were born and bred within its territorial limits and escaped the impress of its characteristics.¶

Of them, Moultrie, Marion, Ramsay, and others have left records, "all of which they saw and part of which they were," that prove the State to have been selfish, cowardly, and treacherous from the beginning.¶

When Prevost appeared off Charleston, in May, 1779, Gov. Rutledge and his council were in the town, and they appointed Gen. Moultrie to command the troops; the same tried soldier who, in June, 1776, had defended the fort on Sullivan's Island, since called by his name. The reader is referred to his "Memoirs of the American Revolution," &c., to learn the particulars of the preliminary struggle between the courage and fidelity of the few and the treachery and cowardice of the many, that culminated in requiring that brave and loyal man to send to the enemy this mean and treasonable message: "To propose a neutrality during the war between Great Britain and America, and the question, whether the State shall belong to Great Britain or remain one of the United States? be determined by the treaty of peace between those two powers." (Memoirs, **[32]**&c., I., 433.)¶

This was the people who had pledged "lives, fortunes and sacred honor" to support the cause of national independence. In the next year the place was ignominiously surrendered to Gen. Clinton and Admiral Arbuthnot, upon compulsion of the same horde of cowards and traitors. The surrender was made May 11, 1780; and so abject and false was the spirit of the people of the State, that only twenty-four days later, June 4, 1780, Sir Henry Clinton could write thus, to Lord George Germaine, one of his Majesty's principal secretaries of state: "With the greatest pleasure I further report to your Lordship, that the inhabitants, from every quarter, repair to the detachments of the army, and to this garrison (Charleston) to declare their allegiance to the king, and to offer their services in arms in support of his government. In many instances they have brought prisoners their former oppressors, or leaders; and I may venture to assert, that there are few men in South Carolina who are not either our prisoners, or in arms with us." (Almon's Remembrancer, X. 76.)¶

On the day after the above was written, June 5, 1780, Clinton and Arbuthnot received an address from "210 principal inhabitants" of Charleston, tendering their "warmest congratulations on the restoration of this capital and province to their political connection with the crown and government of Great Britain." They further said: "When in the progress of that fatal controversy, the doctrine of Independency, which originated in the more northern colonies, made its appearance among us, our nature revolted at the idea, and we look back with the most painful regret on those convulsions that gave existence to a power of subverting a constitution, for which we always had, and ever shall retain, the most profound veneration, and substituting in its stead a rank democracy, which however carefully digested in theory, on being reduced into practice, has exhibited a system of tyrannic domination only to be found among the uncivilized part of mankind, or in the history of the dark and barbarous ages of antiquity." (Almon's Remembrancer, X., 83, 186).¶

How natural that children of such a parentage should fire

upon Fort Sumter and pray for a foreign protectorate! De Kalb expressed his surprise that "so many South Carolinians were **[33]**running to take British protection," and Marion, in explanation, said: "The people of Carolina form two classes, the rich and the poor. The poor are very poor; the rich, who have slaves to do all their work, give them no employment. Unsupported by the rich, they continue poor and low-spirited. The little they get is laid out in brandy, not in books and newspapers; hence they know nothing of the comparative blessings of our country, or of the dangers which threaten it; therefore, they care nothing about it. The rich are generally very rich; afraid to stir lest the British should burn their houses and carry off their negroes." (Weems & Corry's Life of Marion, p. 92.)

It is beyond dispute, that in "the times that tried men's souls," this thoroughly base and treacherous community refused to fight in behalf of the cause, to support which it had pledged everything held sacred among men; but took up arms with alacrity in behalf of the public and foreign enemy, and betrayed, captured, or killed such of their fellow-citizens as remained loyal to the common cause, the faith of the State and their personal honor.¶

The subsequent career of the State harmonizes with its antecedents. As a member of a great political association, receiving protection and owing fealty, its skirts are shamefully free from the stains of conflict with the foes of the common nationality, whether alien or domestic, though solemnly bound to oppose both.¶

But, as a circumscribed political community, unrestrained within its own limits in regard to its economy and institutions, it comes before us "with garments rolled in blood." Without courage or patriotism to encounter a foreign enemy in such warfare as is considered honorable, its people have never hesitated to shed the blood of friends, neighbors, or kindred, to gratify private vengeance. Hence, its domestic annals are rife with street-fights, duels, maimings and assassinations, seldom having any higher oc-

intellect and the fairest character to be found among the adherents of slavery, re-enacted the role of Strafford, and prepared "a Thorough," but escaped his fate. Future generations will not cease to marvel why the most stupendous political criminal of his day received the honors of his country while he lived, and its tears when dead, and will avenge upon his memory the lapses of his cotemporaries. In so conspicuous a career, run by one of so much intellectual power, for such detestable ends, there can be but little to prevent a constant struggle between wonder and disgust.¶

He was the ablest of the few upon earth, who, in the middle of **[35]**the nineteenth century, maintained Slavery upon merits of its own. Against the equities and charities of the religion he professed, and the universal sentiment of the civilized world, he declared it just and kind; against the maxims of political economy, and in full view of the steady impoverishment and exhaustion of the whole slave region, he pronounced it wise and profitable; in presence of a rapid degeneracy in morals and a swift increase of ignorance and barbarism among his people, he contended that the institution was purifying and refining; against the doctrines of the Declaration of Independence and the text and political purposes of the Constitution, he claimed that it existed in right of both, and demanded amendment of the one and repudiation of the other, to reduce Freedom to the imbecility of Slavery, and thus create what he called a balance of power.¶

Himself a husband and father, and personally scorning the traffic, he exacted governmental sanctions that others might pursue it in the wives of other husbands, in the children of other fathers. He lived and died striving to procure a decree that that should be deemed legal and respectable in the waters of the Potomac, which the same judicatory had declared to be piracy in the Bight of Benin; and to perpetuate in the capital of a Christian nation practices which all the religion, all the philanthropy and all the statesmanship of the civilized world, his own country included, were laboring to abolish in Timbuctoo.¶

Naturally enough, under his leading, such a State as his

went steadily from one degree of folly and truculence to another until its name could not be spoken, but "to make the unskillful laugh and the judicious grieve." It may be that the countervailing influences of Slavery would have have rendered [read: would have rendered] nugatory counsels less pernicious than those Mr. Calhoun impressed upon the viciousness and ignorance of his State, but the responsibility is his that the essay was not made.¶

But few of this or any age will come to the bar of posterity so laden with crime against human liberty. It cannot be said when mankind will consent to forget him. If he has won fame, it can be only of the sort from which the good and great recoil with horror. The lustre of his private virtues which even yet dazzles us, will be too dim to blind the eyes of **[36]**a constantly improving posterity to the crimes which darken his public career. If his name is destined to immortality, so it is to infamy, for in this world John C. Calhoun can only be remembered as is "Jeroboam, the son of Nebat, who made Israel to sin."

Rutledge expressed the sentiment of Slavery only, pure and simple; that of the Convention was delivered by George Mason, of Virginia. He said: "The present question concerns not the importing States alone, but the whole Union. Slavery discourages arts and manufactures. The poor despise labor when performed by slaves. They prevent the immigration of whites, who really enrich and strengthen a country. They produce a most pernicious effect on manners. Every master of slaves is born a petty tyrant. They bring the judgment of heaven on a country. As nations cannot be rewarded or punished in the next world, they must be in this. By an inevitable chain of causes and effects, Providence punishes national sins by national calamities."¶

He lamented that some of our Eastern brethren had, from lust of gain, embarked in this nefarious traffic. As to the States being in possession of the right to import, this was the case with many other rights, now to be properly given up. He held it essential, in every point of view, that ["]the General Government should have power to prevent the increase of slavery." (Madison Papers, III. 1391.) Has any modern abolitionist done more than re-affirm and elaborate these views of Mason?

The Northern States were influenced to consent to the license of the Slave trade, by the circumstance that with it would be granted to Congress power to regulate the commerce of the country, which they considered vital to their interests. To Slavery, for its own sake, no such thing would have been conceded. Few were interested in the profits of the Slave trade, but all were in those of Commerce. Hildreth says: "Thus by an understanding, or as Gouverneur Morris called it, 'a bargain' between the commercial representative[s] of the Northern States and the delegates from South Carolina and Georgia, and in spite of the opposition of Maryland and Virginia, the unrestricted power of Congress to pass navigation laws, was con-**[37]**ceded to the Northern merchants, and to the Carolina rice planters, as an equivalent, twenty years' continuance of the African Slave Trade.¶

"This was the third great compromise of the Constitution. The other two were the concessions to the smaller States of an equal representation in the Senate, and, to the slaveholders, the counting of three-fifths of the slaves in determining the ratio of representation. If this third compromise differed from the other two by involving not only a political but a moral sacrifice, there was this partial compensation about it, that it was not permanent, like the others, but expired at the end of twenty years by its own limitation." (Hist. U. S., III., 520.)

Notwithstanding this temporary infidelity to religion and humanity, the Framers did not relax their purpose to make the Constitution, in perpetuity, a defence to Freedom and a barrier to Slavery. They did, indeed, wink at the probable introduction of slaves for a season, but not for an instant would they "admit in the Constitution, the idea that there could be property in man." Hence, they said: "The emigration or importation of such persons," &c., covering the wretched victims of the traffic with the mantle of personality [personalty]; and ample enough was the garment as they made it.¶

The Convention further illustrated its meaning, by refusing to levy a duty upon them as merchandise; and again marked its appreciation of their character, and exhibited its willingness to discourage the commerce, by authorizing a duty or tax upon them, "not exceeding ten dollars for each *person."* Gouverneur Morris called attention to the circumstance that it permitted a tax upon freemen; and George Mason replied, that the tax would be necessary to restrain the importation of convicts. (Madison Papers, III., 1429-30.)¶

Every human being of whom the Constitution took cognizance; was a person, black or white, bond or free, and by the foreordained purpose of its Framers, it is without any faculty whatever to discern distinctions founded upon color or condition.

It is an admitted characteristic of apostates to surpass in malignity and baseness the natural enemies of the cause they have betrayed. This depraved class among us is accustomed to represent, the Constitution and its cotemporaneous history, **[38]**and especially the causes of the present civil war, under aspects totally false and deceptive; and so characterized indeed by the more intelligent and frank of the very traitors in whose interest such falsehoods are forged. Such rebels as Vice-President Stephens, Gov. Hammond, and Mr. Spratt, stigmatize their representations as opposed to truth; still the mendacious creatures persist in tendering their despised tribute and accept with complacency the scorn and rebuke of men, who, although wicked enough to maintain rebellion against the "best government the world ever saw," yet are not abandoned enough to accept such aid even in behalf of the worst of all causes.¶

The first named, by general consent the ablest man in the Confederacy, commending its Constitution said : "The new Constitution has put at rest forever all the agitating questions relating to our peculiar institution—African Slavery as it exists among us—

the proper *status* of the negro in our form of civilization. *This was the immediate cause of the late rupture and present revolution.*¶

"Jefferson, in his forecast, had anticipated this as 'the rock upon which the old Union would split.' He was right. What was conjecture with him, is now a realized fact. But whether he fully comprehended the great truth upon which that rock stood and stands, may be doubted. *The prevailing ideas entertained by him, and most of the leading statesmen at the time of the formation of the old Constitution, were that the enslavement of the African was in violation of the laws of nature; that it was wrong in principle, socially, morally, and politically.* It was an evil they knew not well how to deal with, *but the general opinion of the men of that day was,* that somehow or other, in the order of Providence, *the institution would be evanescent and pass away. This idea, though not incorporated in the Constitution, was the prevailing idea at the time.* The Constitution, it is true, secured every essential guaranty to the institution while it should last, and hence no argument can be justly used against the constitutional guarantees thus secured, because of the common sentiment of the day. These ideas, however, were fundamentally wrong. They rested upon an assumption of the equality of races. This was an error. It was a sandy foundation, and the idea of a government built upon it—when 'the **[39]**storm came, and the wind blew, it fell.' *Our new government is founded upon exactly the opposite ideas; its foundations are laid, its corner-stone rests upon the great truth that the negro is not equal to the white man; that slavery, subordination to the superior race, is his natural and normal condition. This, our new government, is the first, in the history of the world, based upon this great physical, philosophical, and moral truth."* (Speech at Savannah. Rebellion Rec., Vol. I., p. 45.)

This very candid testimony of the second officer of the Confederacy, that Mr. Jefferson and "most of the leading statesmen, at the time of the formation of the old Constitution," regarded slavery as a "violation of the laws of nature," and "wrong in principle, socially, morally, and politically," and that "the general opinion of the men of that day" was, that "the institution would be evanescent and pass away," is creditable to him; seeing the cause he had at heart might well have borne the suppression of the facts in this particular, though his character as a man of truth might not.¶

The appropriation of undefined "constitutional guarantees" to the behoof of Slavery, might be expected from any man occupying the position he did. It has been shown, however, that no recognition of Slavery was designed by the Convention, or granted by the Constitution, nor could men, of the sentiments described by Mr. Stephens, have given to Slavery, under any aspect, guarantees that would conflict with the ultimate right intended to be, and as the Convention supposed, actually was reserved to the General Government.¶

Slavery and the Slave Trade were regarded as coterminous by all at that day, and especially by the northern delegates, who exchanged their votes for a license to the Slave Trade for southern votes in favor of granting to Congress supreme control over the commerce of the country. More than one conscience was salved by the belief that when the one ceased by limitation, the other would perish by inanition. The cogency of Oliver Ellsworth's plea, in behalf of South Carolina and Georgia, resides in the fact, that so deadly was the character of their rice swamps, that the institution could only be maintained by "foreign supplies" of slaves. Even in him there was a substratum of belief; that, "the institution would be evanescent and pass away." **[40]**"Slavery, in time," said he, "will not be a speck in our country." To his colleague, Roger Sherman, "the abolition of Slavery seemed to be going on in the United States, and the good sense of the several States would probably, by degrees, soon complete it." By faith he saw the end of Slavery, and not far off. No mercenary or timeserver among the delegates thought he was doing worse than postponing the extinction of Slavery twenty years, by consenting to this license.

Since 1808, however, the General Government has been in

gates. Slavery, in its essence, seems to have "given up" the right with remarkable composure. It protested and demanded with earnestness, but what? that the right should not be exercised within twenty years—nothing else. As against the right, it said nothing; against a premature exercise of it, much. And the Convention consented and agreed, not to the remission or abrogation of the right, but that it might slumber for twenty years; at the expiration of which, both Slavery and the Convention expected the General Government to "awake to righteousness" and "prevent the increase of Slavery."¶

What a talent this nation received and buried in the earth? [Read: earth!] how much longer will it abstain from putting to use this trust, that an Austere Master, at his coming, may receive "his own with usury?" When the amendments to the Constitution, now pending, shall become part and parcel of "the supreme law of the land," and human slavery is forever prohibited, the original and true intent of the Constitution will be executed and an error of judgment on the part of the Framers corrected—nothing more. No compromise or understanding with men will have suffered any violence whatever, and a high duty to God and man will be no longer undischarged.

The utmost that can be claimed as favoring Slavery, however disguised, in virtue of the action of the Convention, is, that to secure the ratification of the Constitution by two States, and to Congress the supreme control of the commerce of the country, it conceded to the Anthropophagi of South Carolina and Georgia liberty to protract their feast for still twenty years; taking care the while, that the viands should be "persons"—not slaves. Also, that persons held to "service or labor," in a manner specified, might be reclaimed in cases of escape.

On the other hand, as against Slavery, it enfranchised three-fifths of all its chattels, to the extent of making slaves as truly subjects of representation in the Federal councils as their owners. **[42]**That slaves did not succeed to the right of voting for their own representatives was in nowise by the act or omission of the Convention, but is due wholly to the iniquity of legislation within the States over which it had no control. It declared and acted, throughout, upon the assumption that in contemplation of Federal law and Federal administration, slaves were "persons," not separable from the mass of the population, and refused to take cognizance of them in any other aspect. It forbore to make color a condition or element of either personality [personalty] or citizenship.

In the presence of such conditions both of law and fact, Chief Justice Taney came to the conclusions announced in his opinion in the Dred Scott case. Some of them are quite remarkable. He says:

> "In the opinion of the court, the legislation and histories of the times, and the language used in the Declaration of Independence, show, that neither the class of persons who had been imported as slaves, nor their descendants, whether they had become free or not, were then acknowledged as a part of the people, nor intended to be included in the general words used in that memorable instrument.
>
> "It is difficult at this day to realize the state of public opinion in relation to that unfortunate race, which prevailed in the civilized and enlightened portions of the world at the time of the Declaration of Independence, and when the Constitution of the United States was framed and adopted. But the public history of every European nation displays it in a manner too plain to be mistaken.
>
> "They had for more than a century before been regarded as beings of an inferior order, and altogether unfit to associate with the white race, either in social or political relations; and so far inferior, that they had no rights which the white man was bound to respect; and that the negro might justly and lawfully be reduced to slavery for his benefit. He was bought and sold, and treated as an ordinary article of merchandise and traffic, whenever a profit could be made by it. This opinion was at that time fixed and universal in

> the civilized portion of the white race. It was regarded as an axiom in morals as well as in politics, which no one thought of disputing, or supposed to be open to dispute; and men in every grade and position in society daily and habitually acted upon it in their private pursuits, as well as in matters of public concern, without doubting for a moment the correctness of this opinion.
>
> "And in no nation was this opinion more firmly fixed or more uniformly acted upon than by the English Government and English people. They not only seized them on the coast of Africa, and sold them or held them in Slavery for their own use, but they took them as ordinary articles of merchandise to every country where they could make a profit on them, and were far more extensively engaged in this commerce than any other nation in the world.
>
> "The opinion thus entertained and acted upon in England was naturally impressed upon the colonies they founded on this side of the Atlantic. **[43]**And, accordingly, a negro of the African race was regarded by them as an article of property, and held, and bought, and sold as such, in every one of the thirteen colonies which united in the Declaration of Independence, and afterwards formed the Constitution of the United States. The slaves were more or less numerous in the different colonies, as slave labor was found more or less profitable. But no one seems to have doubted the correctness of the prevailing opinion of the time."

Who, giving faith to these statements of the Chief Justice, could come to any other conclusion than that African Slavery was a pet institution of the whole civilized world at the time of the Revolution, and when the present Constitution was adopted? That, in contemplation of law and morals, the negro was everywhere regarded as property; but especially so by the Government and people of England, and that the same opinion "was naturally impressed upon the colonies they founded on this side of the Atlantic?" Enough of the history of those times has been already quoted to show these statements to be false in respect to his own country, and they are not less so in respect to the "civilized and enlightened portions" of the rest of the world, and most especially, England.¶

Northington, Mansfield, every jurist of that country who had spoken with authority, pronounced the institution odious, infamous, and utterly opposed to the laws of the realm. It is well known that Lord Mansfield would gladly have decided otherwise had either the laws or sentiment of England permitted him; that he did not, with his strong bias, shows how positive on the point was both law and opinion in that kingdom.

It is, however, as a libeler of the purest age of the Republic and of the best men the country has produced, that the Chief Justice is conspicuously false and malignant. His high position, officially, so inconsistent with that he chose to assume, and the distrust that attaches to the opinions of unfriendly cotemporaries, make it fortunate that he stands convicted by the very record to which he appealed, in the present judgment of such as love Slavery as he did, but love truth as he did not.¶

Not a respectable man of the Revolutionary or the Constitutional epoch held the views attributed to them by the Chief Justice. Every man of mark among them, except perhaps the impious Rutledge, and one or two of his colleagues, has bequeathed to **[44]**us such memorials of his constant and unappeasable hatred of the institution, on grounds social, moral and political, that the statement of the Chief Justice to the contrary is not less remarkable for boldness than falsehood.¶

Alexander H. Stephens is, indeed, audacious enough to dispute the soundness of the sentiment of the men and the times named by the Chief Justice, but shrinks from the turpitude of denying that such views prevailed. He seems ready and willing to shipwreck his reputation as a statesman on an idea false in morals and economy; but spares his honor as a private person, by forbearing to take the false side in an issue of fact—quite capable of believing a lie, not capable of telling one.

In 1818, as has been shown, Mr. Taney regarded Slavery as an institution *"imposed* upon us by another nation, while yet we were in a state of colonial vassalage;" which does not very well consist with his more recent allegations, that the justice and lawfulness of negro slavery was "regarded as an axiom in morals as well as in politics, which no one thought of disputing or supposed to be open to dispute;" and that the opinions entertained and acted upon in England, were "naturally impressed upon the colonies they founded on this side of the Atlantic." At that time, in his judgment, it was "a hard necessity, indeed," that compelled us to "endure the evils of Slavery for a time;" and that, while it continued, it was "a blot on our national character," that "every real lover of Freedom confidently" hoped would be effectually wiped away, and earnestly looked for the means by which that "necessary object" would be attained; and that, until it was accomplished, and the time came," when we could point without a blush to the language held in the Declaration of Independence, every friend of humanity seek to lighten the galling chain of Slavery, and better, to the utmost of his power, the wretched condition of the slave." He then insisted upon "the principles contained in that venerated instrument."¶

Now, after thirty-eight years more of the experience of the evils of Slavery, and by consequence of the benefits of free institutions, he again invoked the sanctions of that "venerated instrument."

His purpose, as stated by himself, was "to determine **[45]**whether the general terms used in the Constitution of the United States as to the rights of man and the rights of the people was intended to include them, or to give to them or their posterity the benefit of any of its provisions;" meaning by them and their, Africans and the descendants of Africans; and he pronounces the language of the Declaration "conclusive" on the point, as indeed it is.¶

After quoting the memorable plea, put in on behalf of all mankind, beginning "We hold these truths to be self-evident, that all men are created equal," &c., the Chief Justice proceeds to controvert those self-evident truths, and to impeach both the intelligence and integrity of men who, in the next paragraph, are characterized by him as "great men, high in literary acquirements, high in their sense of honor, and incapable of asserting principles inconsistent with those on which they were acting." He says :

> "The general words above quoted would seem to embrace the whole human family, and if they were used in a similar instrument at this day would be so understood. But it is too clear for dispute that the enslaved African race were not intended to be included, and formed no part of the people who framed and adopted this Declaration; for, if the language, as understood in that day, would embrace them, the conduct of the distinguished men who framed the Declaration of Independence would have been utterly and flagrantly inconsistent with the principles they asserted; and instead of the sympathy of mankind, to which they so confidently appealed, they would have deserved and received universal rebuke and reprobation."

There never has been the day, neither before, at the time, nor since the Revolution, when the words "all men" meant anything else than they do "at this day," and will continue to mean, so long as the English language may be preserved. The Chief Justice ignores a fact, too notorious for him not to have known it, that if the power of the Continental Congress had been commensurate with its will, no case like that of Dred Scott would have cursed him with opportunity to reveal himself as ready to falsify the history of his country as to violate its Constitution for the maintenance of so infamous an institution.¶

Much more than the Constitutional Convention was it without jurisdiction to conform the actual condition of "all men" to that which it declared to be their rightful one; but so far as the circumstances of the time permitted it did go and pro-**[46]**claimed the natural equality of all men, without any reservation whatever.¶

The baneful prerogatives and immunities claimed in virtue of State Rights, had not then been formally surrendered; they were still crude though in a crucible and certain to be fused. They

their oracles, his own **[47]**face had become as brass, while all the loyal and humane throughout the land and world were blushing for him.

At forty, Mr. Taney had responded to the call of the Revolution; "insisted on the principles contained in that venerated instrument," the Declaration; shared in the belief of the period, that "the evils of Slavery" were to be endured "for a time" only; "confidently" hoped, and "earnestly" looked for the means, by which that "necessary object" might be attained; and declared it to be, meanwhile, the duty of "every friend of humanity," to "seek to lighten the galling chain of Slavery, and better, to the utmost of his power, the wretched condition of the slave." At eighty, clothed with the power and prerogative of the most potential place in the nation, on an occasion when he might have promoted, essentially, a consummation for which nearly the whole earth was panting, he proved false to himself, false to the hopes and charities he had once cherished, false to the liberal principles he had eulogized, and to a Free Constitution he had sworn to support, and misused the mighty influences of his office to make "the blot on our national character" indelible; to case-harden "the galling chain of Slavery," and to put forever beyond redemption, "the wretched condition of the slave."

The stress of his case required the Chief Justice to apply the same process to the Constitution that he had to the Declaration. It is painful to contemplate the recklessness, even, with which he applies them. He says:

> "But there are two clauses in the Constitution which point directly and specifically to the negro race as a separate class of persons, and show clearly that they were not regarded as a portion of the people or citizens of the Government then formed."

Now, there are not "two clauses," nor any clauses, in the Constitution, "which point directly and specifically to the negro race as a separate class of persons;" nor which point to that race at all, for any purpose whatever, except for exactly the opposite of that alleged by the Chief Justice. So far as the "two clauses" relied upon are concerned, they refute the allega-**[48]**tion by their own text, and invert both the fact and the inference stated by the Chief Justice. He betrays his own consciousness, that his pretence could not confront the simple and significant language of the Constitution, by describing, instead of quoting these important provisions, thus:

> "One of these clauses reserves to each of the thirteen States, the right to import slaves until the year 1808, if it thinks proper. And the importation which it thus sanctions, was unquestionably of persons of the race of which we are speaking, as the traffic in slaves in the United States had always been confined to them. And by the other provision the States pledge themselves to each other to maintain the right of property of the master, by delivering up to him any slave who may have escaped from his service, and be found within their respective territories. By the first above-mentioned clause, therefore, the right to purchase and hold this property is directly sanctioned and authorized for twenty years by the people who framed the Constitution. And by the second, they pledge themselves to maintain and uphold the right of the master in the manner specified, as long as the Government they then formed should endure. And these two provisions show, conclusively, that neither the description of persons therein referred to, nor their descendants, were embraced in any of the other provisions of the Constitution; for certainly these two clauses were not intended to confer on them or their posterity the blessings of liberty, or any of the personal rights so carefully provided for the citizen."

In regard to the right reserved by the clause first mentioned, it may be remarked, that whatever its nature, it was partial in its grant and limited in its term. No State not then existing, could use the right at all. No State then existing, could use it after the lapse of twenty years. Thus if by any construction it might, during its term, have militated against the political privileges or the *status* of any class of persons, it is manifest that there was no purpose to suffer any resulting disability to survive the provision that caused it, nor any possibility of such a result.

It cannot be necessary to repeat what has been said of this least respectable clause of the Constitution. It defies justification, and being dead, one could wish it were buried out of sight. It will not do, however, to suffer its carcass, bereft of vitality since 1808, to become an agency of more extended and enduring wrong, than it was in its day of life and power.¶

Bad as it unquestionably was, it was never the infamous thing represented by the Chief Justice. If he had charged that "those **[49]**reptiles who live by trading in human flesh, and enrich themselves by tearing the husband from the wife, the infant from the bosom of the mother," had prosecuted their dreadful traffic under it, it could not have been denied; but it would be difficult to express an equal sum of falsehood in so few words as the Chief Justice does in these, that it "reserves to each of the thirteen States the right to import slaves;" unless that feat be not only equaled, but surpassed, by the further statement, that by virtue of this clause "the right to purchase and hold this property is directly sanctioned and authorized for twenty years by the people who framed the Constitution."¶

The Constitution reserved no right of any sort to any State, in strict truth, though that mode of expressing the effect of this provision has been accepted; still, as we are dealing with the matter at this point, it is proper to say, that what the Constitution really did, was to covenant with the existing States not to exercise a right of its own within twenty years. The right thus put in abeyance for twenty years, was the right "to prevent the increase of Slavery;" which object, as was then supposed by all parties, would be accomplished whenever "the migration or importation" of certain persons should be prohibited. So far from sanctioning or encouraging the commerce anticipated, "the people who framed the Constitution," discouraged and restrained it so far as they could, by imposing upon the subjects thereof a duty or tax "not exceeding ten dollars for each person."

It requires much self-denial to speak with moderation of an attempt to found a proposition subversive of a fundamental principle and main object of the Constitution, upon a temporary and occasional provision of the instrument, never operative but to a carefully limited extent, and for the preceding eight and forty years, wholly inert and powerless. But the deliberate and elaborate misrepresentation of such a provision, in the precise aspect in which it has been debated and passed upon by "the people who framed the Constitution," is still harder to bear from a quarter whence truth, in matters of fact at least, might fairly be expected. That this clause did not "point directly and specifically to the negro race," and did point to the white race as well, is the identical fact Gouverneur Morris pre-**[50]**sented to the attention of the Convention; and George Mason's commentary convicts the Chief Justice of something, which, it is to be feared, is not ignorance. Mason admitted the obvious truth, that it did include white as well as black; and commended it, by alleging its usefulness to prevent the importation of convicts, whom no one supposed would be negroes or slaves. No man in or out of the Convention, then or since, ever supposed the provision to include less. Of this there is abundant evidence.

In 1798, the Legislature of Kentucky took action in regard to the celebrated Alien and Sedition Laws, and passed the famous Resolutions, understood to have been written by Mr. Jefferson. One of them is in these words:

> "V. *Resolved,* That in addition to the general principle as well as the express declaration, that powers not delegated are reserved, another and more special provision, inserted in the Constitution from abundant caution, has declared, 'that the migration or importation of such persons as any of the States now existing shall think proper to admit, shall not be prohibited by the Congress prior to the year 1808.' That this Commonwealth does admit the migration of alien friends described as the subject of the said act concerning aliens; that a provision against prohibiting their migration is a provision against all acts equivalent thereto, or it would be nugatory; that to remove them when migrated is equivalent to a pro-

hibition of their migration, and is therefore contrary to the said provision of the Constitution, and void."

It has never been claimed that the laws in question were aimed, specially, at the negro race; yet the very clause, which the Chief Justice affirmed "pointed directly and specifically" to that race, was appealed to, while it was operative, by such men as Mr. Jefferson and the legislators of Kentucky, to protect white men against the force of those laws. It could be wished that the Chief Justice might explain, in this connection, why his intendment, that the persons referred to by this clause were negroes, and slaves because they were such, did not apply with equal propriety to the subjects of the act concerning aliens?

The second provision fares no better than the first named under the manipulation of the Chief Justice. From this provision, amended again and again by the Convention, for the avowed purpose that "the idea that there could be property in **[51]**man" might receive no countenance from it, this wretched alchemist distils the essence of the contrary doctrine. He declares that, by it, "the States pledge themselves to each other to maintain the right of property in the master" and "the people who framed the Constitution" also "pledge themselves to uphold the right of the master, in the manner specified, so long as the Government they then formed should endure."¶

If it has not been shown, conclusively, that these deductions of the Chief Justice, are, "directly and specifically," at war with the facts in the case, and with every inference justified by them, there is no force in the truth of history nor in the meaning of language.

The Chief Justice took no better care of his intellectual reputation than of his judicial and moral character. He did not scruple to utter from the bench logic like this; trusting to the popular respect for his office to give it effect in the non-professional world outside. He says:

"And these two provisions show, conclusively, that neither the description of persons therein referred to, nor their descendants, were embraced in any of the other provisions of the Constitution; for certainly these two clauses were not intended to confer on them or their posterity the blessings of liberty, or any of the personal rights so carefully provided for the citizen."

On any other occasion, or for any other purpose, the Chief Justice could hardly have failed to hold that the nature and effect of "the other provisions of the Constitution" must be determined by the text of the provisions themselves, and not by that of some other provisions of no superior authority. If the sum of all the provisions, in a given case, was ten, it would be a novelty, even in injustice, to prove the character of eight of them by what might be found in the other two; and this, too, when the eight were in presence and as amenable to examination as the two subjected to that process.¶

In the case supposed, there would be no evidence that the eight, assumed, from the analysis of the two, to be altogether destitute of a certain element, were not, in point of fact, made up of that precise thing, wholly, or chiefly. The mode of reasoning resorted to by the Chief Justice, so far as conformity to the rules of construction and interpretation, or of common sense is concerned, **[52]**scarcely comes up to the standard of Dogberry; and, in view of his conceded intelligence, no one will believe that he did not know it. In the case in question, if it were quite true, that the "two clauses" did not confer blessings upon the subjects of them, it would not follow that "the other provisions of the Constitution" did not abound in benefits "to them and their posterity."

One of these provisions, certainly, had no concern whatever with any human being then in the country; nor is it easy to conceive how the *status* of any who were here was to be affected by a contingent provision in respect to such as had not arrived and might never come.¶

Neither of the two, however, makes the slightest reference

Seeing the Chief Justice was in pursuit of some provision in the Constitution, which points "directly and specifically to the negro race," it is quite remarkable, that he overlooked the only one in regard to which it might be true, and found two, in respect to which, it was positively false.¶

Sec. 2, Art. III., of the Constitution, says: "Representatives and direct taxes shall be apportioned among the several States which may be included within this Union, according to their respective numbers, which shall be determined by adding to the whole number of free persons, including those bound to service for a term of years, and, excluding Indians, not taxed, three-fifths of all other persons."

It was not concealed at the time that the "three-fifths of all other persons" named in this article, were of the class referred to by the Chief Justice, and it had been applied to them in practice from that time to the hour in which he was speaking. The doctrine that no power in the Constitution, save that contained in the "two clauses," can rightfully be exercised, "in relation to this race," makes a sorry figure in presence of the fact that the General Government, from its foundation, has recognized and acted under the power contained in the article quoted. Not a Congress has ever sat under the Constitution that did not represent the "three-fifths of all other persons."¶

The precious right to be represented in the public councils, is secured by the Constitution to the "three-fifths," in the same terms and to the same extent that it is to all other persons who enjoy it, the Chief Justice himself included. It was not more perfect nor more extended in his case than in theirs; and if he had been required to show the ground of his own right in this behalf, he could have found it only in the same muniment and the same **[54]**words that granted theirs. If he had sought why it was that he enjoyed privileges incident to the right, and they did not, he would have found the Constitution innocent in the matter; and that the sole cause of the difference resided in inequitable legislation by the several States which defrauded them and spared him.

The Chief Justice resolutely refused to see—the most hopeless of all forms of blindness—what the history and text of the Constitution make conspicuous as "a city set on a hill," that the gist of the compromise then made between Freedom and Slavery was, that in all exhibitions of the National presence, the one should conceal from the view of beholders every feature inconsistent with the aspect the other was bound to exhibit before the world. Slavery, for considerations satisfactory to itself, had consented and agreed to do this; but the Chief Justice declined to be bound by the arrangement, or to recognize the fact that both parties had at once proceeded to act upon the understanding, and that it was still subsisting while he was repudiating instead of maintaining it.¶

Was it for any other reason that Slavery was not allowed to import a slave, to reclaim a slave, nor to represent a slave, except that in [read: that, except in] the "form and pressure" of persons, or, if it be insisted on, under the fiction that they were such, and not in anywise distinguishable from the mass of the population, the Constitution neither could nor would recognize or protect them at all? Chattels, these "three-fifths" might be held to be in some jurisdiction, alien and hostile to Freedom; but manhood, not chattelhood, was an inexorable condition to entitle them to the regard of her Constitution.¶

In respect to right and capacity to be represented, the Constitution makes no distinction between such as affect to be masters and those whom they claim are their slaves. In the view of the Constitution they stand upon a common level. The right conceded is common to both, and is as complete and operative in the one as in the other. Neither can be divested of it. The so-called slaves are as competent to demand it as the so-called masters—their rights in this behalf are precisely equal, and neither has the slightest right to disfranchise the other, nor **[55]**themselves, either. The entire constituency is homogeneous in the contemplation of the Constitution.

Slavery was wiser in accepting manhood as its "image and superscription" in the superior and protecting jurisdiction, than the Chief Justice was in obliterating it. While the arrangement was adhered to, chattelhood reposed safely in its burrows, and to all human appearance, might have long continued to do so. Upon the encouragement of the Chief Justice, it saw fit to leave its retreats, and now it is scarcely among the things possible on earth that it can ever regain them.

Most of the questions raised by the Chief Justice, had been settled by the practice of the country before the Constitution was made; and all that the instrument did, was to accept and re-execute such settlements. Prominent among them is one, which is also the main one in the Dred Scott case, of the novelty and importance of which, the Chief Justice professed to be aware. He says:

> "This is certainly a very serious question, and one that now for the first time has been brought for decision before this Court. But it is brought here by those who have a right to bring it, and it is our duty to meet it and decide it.
>
> "The question is simply this: Can a negro, whose ancestors were imported into this country, and sold as slaves, become a member of the political community formed and brought into existence by the Constitution of the United States, and as such become entitled to all the rights and privileges, and immunities guarantied by that instrument to the citizen? One of which rights is the privilege of sueing in a court of the United States in the cases specified in the Constitution."

It might have occurred to one much less astute than the Chief Justice, that there was enough to put one on his guard in the very fact that it had never before been raised. The country had possessed negroes, Chief Justices and Courts, as long as it had the Constitution, and also citizens who had a "right to bring" such questions; yet, for nearly three score years and ten, with the institutions of the country in perpetual motion, no occasion had arisen for a citizen to trouble a Chief Justice with any such question. During the term, say of sixty-nine years, some practice or other had obtained, and any doctrine adverse to our current, for so long a season, needed to rest **[56]**on a very sure foundation. He might have suspected even that in the absence of such Chief Justices as himself, the question might have slumbered sixty-nine years longer.

It was too much even for the Chief Justice to claim, as matter of law, that any who were citizens when the Constitution was made, ceased to be so by reason of its adoption. He disclaims this with almost a flourish of frankness. He says:

> "It is true, every person, and every class and description of persons, who were at the time of the adoption of the Constitution recognized as citizens in the several States, became also citizens of this new political body; "—

But after making the admission, he undertakes to establish. as matter of fact, that so impossible a result did actually follow; and then, to justify it by judicial construction of the Constitution. To seem to do this required mis-statement of fact and perversion of law; but as it could be done in no other way, and Slavery, as he supposed, needed that it be done, the Chief Justice set about it without scruple or remorse.

Mr. Justice Curtis, in his dissenting opinion, exposes many mis-statements of fact and erroneous conclusions of law, which are main supports of the opinion of the Chief Justice. The limits of this notice forbid the extended quotations it would be grateful to make; but let no layman suppose himself acquainted with the enormities contained in the opinion of the Chief Justice, until he shall have read the dissenting opinions in the case, and especially the luminous and decisive one of Mr. Justice Curtis.

Mr. Justice Curtis says:

> "To determine whether any free persons, descended from

Africans held in Slavery, were citizens of the United States under the Confederation, and consequently at the time of the adoption of the Constitution of the United States, it is only necessary to know whether any such persons were citizens of either of the States under the Confederation, at the time of the adoption of the Constitution.

"Of this there can be no doubt. At the time of the ratification of the Articles of Confederation, all free native-born inhabitants of the States of New Hampshire, Massachusetts, New York, New Jersey, and North Carolina, though descended from African slaves, were not only citizens of those states, but such of them as had the other necessary qualifications possessed the franchise of electors, on equal terms with other citizens.

[57]"The Supreme Court of North Carolina, in the case of the State *v.* Manuel (4 Dev. and Bat., 20), has declared the law of the State on this subject, in terms which I believe to be as sound law in the other States I have enumerated, as it was in North Carolina.

"'According to the laws of this State,' says Judge Gaston, in delivering the opinion of the Court, all human beings within it, who are not slaves, fall within one of two classes. Whatever distinctions may have existed in the Roman laws between citizens and free inhabitants, they are unknown to our institutions. Before our Revolution, all free persons born within the dominions of the King of Great Britain, whatever their color or complexion, were native-born British subjects—those born out of his allegiance were aliens. Slavery did not exist in England, but it did in the British colonies. Slaves were not in legal parlance persons, but property. The moment the incapacity, the disqualification of Slavery, was removed, they became persons, and were then either British subjects, or not British subjects, according as they were or were not born within the allegiance of the British King. Upon the Revolution, no other change took place in the laws of North Carolina than was consequent on the transition from a colony dependent on a European King, to a free and sovereign State. Slaves remained slaves. British subjects of North Carolina became North Carolina freemen. Foreigners, until made members of the State, remained aliens. Slaves, manumitted here, became freemen, and therefore, if born within North Carolina, are citizens of North Carolina, and all free persons born within the State are born citizens of the State. The Constitution extended the elective franchise to every freeman who had arrived at the age of twenty-one, and paid a public tax; and it is a matter of universal notoriety, that, under it, free persons, without regard to color, claimed and exercised the franchise, until it was taken from free men of color a few years since by our amended Constitution.'

"The Constitution of New Hampshire conferred the elective franchise upon 'every inhabitant of the State having the necessary qualifications,' of which color or descent was not one.

"The Constitution of New York gave the right to vote to 'every male inhabitant, who shall have resided,' &c.; making no discrimination between free colored persons and others. (See Con. of N. Y., Art. 2, Rev. Stats. of N. Y., vol. 1, p. 126.)

"That of New Jersey, to 'all inhabitants of this colony, of full age, who are worth £50 proclamation money, clear estate.'

"New York, by its Constitution of 1820, required colored persons to have some qualifications as prerequisites for voting, which white persons need not possess. And New Jersey, by its present Constitution, restricts the right to vote to white male citizens. But these changes can have no other effect upon the present inquiry, except to show, that before they were made, no such restriction existed; and colored, in common with white persons, were not only citizens of those States, but entitled to the elective franchise on the same qualifications as white persons, as they now are in New Hampshire and Massachusetts."

The Chief Justice, with characteristic boldness and unfairness, ventured to impress into his service some enactments of Massachusetts, designed to prevent the *intermarriage* of whites and "negroes, mulattoes, and Indians," in order to favor the idea, that in this, the freest of all the commonwealths, negroes **[58]**were regarded as not entitled to any rights of citizenship. Mr. Justice Curtis, himself a citizen of that State, thus disposes of that essay. He says :

"An argument from speculative premises, however well chosen, that the then state of opinion in the Commonwealth of Massachusetts, was not consistent with the natural rights of the

> from justice,' who alone were excepted, it is clear, that under the Confederation, and at the time of the adoption of the Constitution, free colored persons of African descent might be, and, by reason of their citizenship in certain States, were entitled to the privileges and immunities of general citizenship of the United States."

To maintain that colored persons have no right under the Constitution but to be slaves, required the Chief Justice to deny that any such persons had lot or part in causing it to be made; **[59]**though the fact was notoriously otherwise. Of the sixty thousand of this class, who were free persons before and at the time the Constitution was made, he coolly disposes, thus:

> "The number that had been emancipated at that time, were but few in comparison with those held in Slavery; and they were identified in the public mind with the race to which they belonged, and regarded as a part of the slave population rather than the free."

Sixty thousand, in the judgment of some, may be a small number contrasted with seven hundred thousand, still it is not small in itself. An army of that number would be considered respectable in size, even now; one, perhaps not larger, is at this moment, holding up, through Georgia and South Carolina, that banner upon which, let it be hoped, the people of those States will look and be healed.¶

If there had been but one of the class in question, he was entitled to recognition at the hands of the highest judicial officer of the country, seeing that respect is due to rights rather than numbers. If so loose a notion, as is described, had been popular at the time alleged, it was the duty of the Chief Justice to show that his judicial action was controlled by more equitable and intelligent views of the fact; and he would appear in an attitude infinitely more becoming, exhibiting deference to the Constitutional rights of a solitary human being, than he does in contemning those of sixty thousand. There is no reason to suppose that the idea in question was ever entertained by any but the Chief Justice; that it was not, at the time stated by him, is abundantly proved by the records and events of that day.¶

Mr. Justice Curtis refutes the statement, and the conclusion drawn from it, triumphantly. He says:

> "It has been often asserted that the Constitution was made exclusively by and for the white race. It has already been shown that in five of the thirteen original States, colored persons then possessed the elective franchise, and were among those by whom the Constitution was ordained and established. If so, it is not true, in point of fact, that the Constitution was made exclusively by the white race. And that it was made exclusively for the white race is, in my opinion, not only an assumption not warranted by anything in the Constitution, but contradicted by its opening declaration, that it was ordained and established by the people of the United States, for themselves and their posterity. And as free colored persons were then citizens of at least five States, and so in every sense part of the people of the United States, they were among those for whom and whose posterity the Constitution was ordained and established."

[60]The learned Justice might have gone farther, and claimed that the class disfranchised so contemptuously by the Chief Justice, was concerned as well in adopting the Constitution after it was made. Who was there, for example, in North Carolina, not represented by the Convention that ratified and adopted the Federal Constitution? The ratifying ordinance, passed November 21, 1789, was in the form of a resolution, and in these words:

> "*Resolved,* That this Convention, in behalf of the freemen, citizens, and inhabitants of the State of North Carolina, do adopt and ratify the said Constitution and form of Government."

Color, as a disqualification for citizenship, is not so much as hinted at from the beginning to the end of the Constitution, yet the Chief Justice scanning it, found it in every line. Unable to rise to the conception that gave the Constitution birth, he strove to degrade it to the level of his own. Not comprehending the almost divine sense of right and justice that constrains the Constitution to behold, "with equal eye," all mankind within its scope, no matter with what color it has pleased the Almighty to tinge them, he regarded this great glory as a blot; unconscious that to him it was "dark with excessive brightness." It is not, as the Chief Justice supposed, color blindness to all colors but one, but a clear perception and an impartial regard for all colors, that characterizes the Constitution.

> "Get thee glass eyes;
> And, like a scurvy politician, seem
> To see things thou dost not,"

is a more practicable counsel, applied to a Chief Justice, than to a Constitution. Still worse would it be, to extinguish sight altogether, under pretence of curing an infirmity of vision.

The most familiar and significant words in our language, if used in the Constitution for the benefit of the negro race, conveyed no meaning to the Chief Justice but one contrary to their general acceptation; and indeed contrary to his own understanding of the same terms in every other relation. The word "person," as used in this connection in the Constitution, **[61]**was perverted by the Chief Justice in a manner and to a degree which exemplifies this habit strikingly. For every purpose and in every connection but this, the most important secular purpose, perhaps, for which the word had ever been used upon earth, it is allowed to mean what it expresses to every human being who understands the English language. The Chief Justice, in his function of expounder of the Constitution, in every case where the word occurs in the instrument, and may, in common with others, include this unfortunate race, defined it to mean "a chattel"—a word that would be well defined, if held to mean "a thing," not to be described by the word "person."¶

No writer, no speaker, no definer of the tongue, ever has attempted a fraud like that upon the meaning of words or the common sense of all who understand them. Again and again did the liberal Constitution baptize these much abused people by the name of persons; and after the lapse of generations, came its High Priest, in his vestments, and upon the altar set up for Liberty, kindled strange fire to consume, not "chattels," nor yet "the blood of bulls and of goats," but the sacred Constitutional rights and franchises of a body of "persons," exceeding in number the whole people who ordained the Constitution, and those of their posterity through all time to come.¶

The entire calendar of judicial malversation will be searched in vain for so shocking an instance as is presented by this malevolent old man, standing with one foot on the bench of the Supreme Court, and the other in the grave, consuming hours so far beyond the promised term of human life that they seem less the closing ones of Time than those of the dawn of Eternity, in the most futile of efforts for the most nefarious of purposes;—to rob one of the most prolific branches of the human family of their natural and constitutional right to be deemed and treated as "persons," then and forever, under a pretence, too feeble to withstand the authority of the horn-book of the school-boy, and frivolous even in the judgment of all above the simplicity of childhood—that, in the Federal Constitution, p-e-r-s-o-n spells property!

In religion, the Chief Justice was Roman Catholic. Bancroft says: "A series of papal bulls had, indeed, secured to the **[62]**Portuguese the exclusive commerce with Western Africa; but the slave trade between Africa and America was, I believe, never expressly sanctioned by the see of Rome. The spirit of the Roman church was against it. Even Leo X., though his voluptuous life, making of his pontificate a continued carnival, might have deadened the sentiments of humanity and justice, declared that 'not the Christian religion only, but nature herself, cries out against the state of Slavery.' and Paul III., in two separate briefs, imprecated a curse on the Europeans who should enslave Indians or any other class of men."¶

This was the voice of that church in the sixteenth century. In the seventeenth, Urban VIII., launched the thunders of the Vatican against the same class of offenders. In 1837, Gregory XVI., served upon the Chief Justice, in common with all Roman Catholics, an injunction, not merely restraining them from buying and selling human beings, but also forbidding each and every of them, "whether ecclesiastical or laical, from presuming to defend that commerce in negro slaves, under pretence or borrowed color, or to teach or publish in any manner, publicly or privately, things contrary" to his admonitions.

If the Chief Justice had abstained from defending "that commerce in negro slaves," or, in order to do so wicked a thing, had forborne to use "pretence or borrowed color," or stolen rather, he would have had the countenance of the standards of his church as well as the sanctions of the Federal Constitution. If the authority of that church had been on the other side, and he had deferred to it, he might then appear obedient as a churchman, though contumacious as a Chief Justice; as it is, he was simply faithless in both relations and unworthy of respect in either.¶

It is an appalling truth, that the demoralization wrought by the influences of human slavery, is the most complete ever witnessed among men. The caustic of all other vices combined does not so thoroughly extirpate from the human mind and conscience every vestige of justice, religion and humanity. Rutledge spoke only the truth when he said, "Religion and humanity have nothing to do with this question." Except they be banished, indeed, there can be no question at all. The annals of crime inform us of highwaymen even, who **[63]**had nothing but pity and benefactions for the oppressed and perishing, while they robbed the rich and powerful without stint or compunction; but the retainers of the "sum of all villainies," unequal to the one virtue of such wrong doers, peril their souls for the profit and security of rich and pampered oppressors of the weak and friendless; and neither exhibit mercy in their lives nor remorse in death, toward those who of all the children of men, are most in need of human sympathy and protection.¶

It would be idle to expect that the mandates of the civil law or of the common conscience could avail in the same jurisdiction where the positive commands of the divine law and the commonest rights of humanity were ostentatiously set aside; or, that the injunctions of a man-made Constitution should have prevailed in a forum where what was believed to be the audible voice of God, and certainly the highest temporal and eternal interests of man, together, pleaded in vain.

If there were some phase of this mournful adjudication, in which the deportment of the Chief Justice might be held to avoid contempt, if it did not challenge respect, the opportunity to present it would not be lost. But it is impossible to discern, either in his personal surroundings or in the general condition of affairs in his own country or throughout the world, anything that threatened to affect the Chief Justice unfavorably, in case he held fast his integrity and independence as a Judge, or as a man, confessed that he was not without the charities that do not always forsake our nature in its lowest estate.¶

The state of civilization, the condition of the law and of public opinion, as well as of the form of religious faith that he professed, all go to increase his condemnation. The tenure of his office defied everything but death or his own misconduct. He might have exhibited, with entire impunity, that low form of courage, which is inspired by the absence of all danger, since not a few of his own vocation had become famous, because they displayed the higher phases of that virtue, in the presence of imminent and deadly peril.¶

He saw fit, too, to apostatize from the "faith and manners" of the most vigorous and creditable time of his life, and as an old man, to commend what he had scorned and denounced in his prime. When, having through a long life proved many **[64]**things and it became, transcendently, his duty to "hold fast that which is good," and to give effect to equitable and generous counsels once

had received him, were his brethren in Christ, used the same "means of grace" and cherished the same "hopes of glory " as himself. The exquisite sense of justice, **[65]**the equal love of humanity, by which Christianity expects to correct the injustice and cruelty of the unregenerate world, received but little illustration from so conspicuous a professor. The light he let shine gilded no such works as, seen of men, constrain them to glorify God and walk in the footsteps of his saints; but rather, resembled that phosphoric glow, which, useless for all purposes of warmth or illumination, only serves to warn beholders to fly it, if they would avoid offence to more delicate senses. He did, nevertheless, turn many faces, and hearts, too, toward the last recourse of human helplessness; but it was to invoke divine protection against his designs and the curse of God upon the most important act of his life. No infidel ever so stirred the church on earth or roused it to such earnest supplication for the direct intervention of its Almighty Head.

As a Jurist, or, more strictly speaking, as a Judge, in which character he will be most remembered, he was, next to Pontius Pilate, perhaps the worst that ever occupied the seat of judgment among men.¶

In denying and mistating notorious matters and conditions of fact, in emasculating and inverting the universal and uncontroverted meaning of simple words, in nullifying and perverting plain provisions of law, and in violating settled rules of evidence and of practice, he equaled Jeffreys, in his worst moods, in his worst days; but in the character and dimensions of his crime against humanity, he infinitely exceeds that monster. The hundreds murdered judicially, and the thousands made to taste "the horrors of the middle passage" in transportation to the Antilles, load Jeffreys with guilt not to be remembered without a shudder; but "the day is coming, perhaps now is," when men will perceive, that the judgment of the Chief Justice surpassed, in cruelty and duration of punishment, any ever pronounced by the infamous Lord Chief Justice, and, indeed, all of them put together.

The axe, the stake or the halter, put a sharp but effectual period to the wrongs and sufferings of many of the victims of Jeffreys; perhaps those were most to be pitied, whom, with superior malignity, he spared from death to undergo a more bitter experience—to feel what, it was to be a slave—the same **[66]**doom affected by the Chief Justice. The descendants of both classes had sad memories indeed of what had been inflicted upon those from whom they derived their being; but neither in their own persons or estates, nor in those of their posterity, was there anything further to be dreaded from the malice and injustice of the vindictive magistrate. The force of that had been expended, mainly, upon the bodies or within the lives of such as had confronted him in life at his own bar; no consequences survived him and them not remediable, at the will of the nation, by Act of Parliament.

Quite otherwise was it with the judgment of the Chief Justice. It was omnipotent and expansive in authority, over the entire jurisdiction to which the American people might attain to the very last hour that the Constitution should endure. He so construed the fundamental law, that the Congress of the nation was impotent to correct his error, however glaring, or to do justice in the premises, however manifest his violation of it; and he wantonly declared void such liberal legislation as it had ordained in the best and purest days the country had ever seen. It was beyond review this side of the court of heaven—final—irrevocable. He fortified his wrong by defences, that the respect of the people for the decisions of their Supreme tribunal, made holy and insuperable.¶

Under this decision, a people old as Noah, numerous as the sands on the seashore, and likely as any other to see the end of the world, as it had its beginning, could neither escape from bondage itself, nor be rescued from it by others, through all time. Ages of birth and residence, of culture and improvement of the soil [read: soul], of service and support of religion, science and learning among the people, not even the salvation of the public liberties, could earn for one of them, rights, which the generous Constitution of the country conferred upon fugitives from all other oppression on the instant they set foot within its jurisdiction. Nether axe, stake or gibbet could appease this insatiable, remorseless judgment. No sum of present anguish could abate its right to extort from the future equal misery. It could neither die nor be satisfied. Not by the shedding of blood could remission be purchased for the sin of having been born of even one colored parent, for thousands **[67]**of them were of such parentage; nor could the sacrifice of every right of man, by every human being of African descent at any one time in the country, have obtained one of the "blessings of liberty," for one child of one of them.¶

Dred Scott would not have exceeded in heroism or devotion, hundreds of his race, then within the jurisdiction of the Court, if he had welcomed death in its most frightful form, to save his children from the fate, which made his life valueless to himself, and then devoted it to the service of another. This judgment made woe congenital in the offspring of millions of men. A condition so void of comfort in the present and of hope in the future, had never been imposed by the vengeance of God on any "kindred tribe or tongue, under the whole heaven;" nor, by the wrath of man.

Striking as the contrast is between the compass and severity of the penalties imposed by them respectively, it is perhaps in the aggregate of their respective victims that the disproportion is calculated to impress most. Reliable records swell the number of those who perished by the fiat of Jeffreys to at least five hundred, many of them wrongfully, and all cruelly; yet this was the least of his enormities, for not less than twice that number he doomed to a fate worse than death—Slavery within the tropics. A fearful array, indeed, to meet in the presence of the Final Judge.¶

Before the Chief Justice appeared a solitary person of African descent, Dred Scott; nor is it likely he was there in any but a technical sense. Probably, he is yet to make the personal acquaintance of the man who judged his cause. Outside of the judgment chamber, but included within the judgment, stood four millions like him, upon every one of whom the eye of the Chief Justice is yet to rest. That comprehensive judgment was instant upon them, and impended over all that might be born of them in the procession of time, and indeed over all of their lineage who might ever find their way to this refuge of the oppressed.¶

The victims of the one were not, in the day of the Coliseum, too many to have been "butchered to make a Roman holiday"—those of the other comprised the present representatives and all the future generations of a people, who were numerous and powerful enough, at that distant day, to **[68]**bring terror to the gates of Rome; and who still hold the grand division of the earth they occupied then. If the one might have depopulated a hamlet, the other would have desolated a continent.

The thanksgiving that has ascended because this fearful judgment failed in accomplishing its purpose, is perhaps as general and fervent as any that ever proceeded from the heart of man.¶

Mingled with thanks to God for so great a deliverance, are ascriptions of praise to men, who, by sympathy or service, aided or welcomed, that benignant result. Among men honored by such remembrances, the Chief Justice does not appear. By no act or consent of his, the fruit of either shame or remorse, did his scheme fail. There is no evidence that he relented of his purpose to the last hour of his life. There are no last words to provoke "men's charitable speeches," or to incline them to regard his tergiversations with that form of charity produced by an infusion of doubt whether they may not be, after all, indications, as well of an infirm head as of an obdurate heart.¶

There is much probability, that, under the increasing clearness of public views of moral and political truth, certain to attend upon a rising and expanding civilization, the memory of the Chief Justice will gather blackness from exposure on the walls of Time; and that the outcry of man against him is destined to increase rather than abate.¶

Perhaps it will not cease, until Dred Scott, and the millions of his co-appellants, shall stand, face to face, with the Chief Justice, at the Grand Assize for all Nations, and an assembled Universe, awed to silence, shall hearken to a review of this judgment, pronounced by the Judge of all the Earth; who, for the warning and instruction of Judges within the jurisdiction of Time, had mercifully advertised them of this canon of the jurisprudence of Eternity:—"For with what judgment ye judge, ye shall be judged; and with what measure ye mete, it shall be measured to you again."

his own, he misused a rare opportunity in order to make them void in a most sacred and powerful jurisdiction, over which he had been set for exactly opposite purposes.¶

As a man, a Christian and a jurist, he falls below the lowest standard of humanity, religion and law, recognized among civilized men.

As a man, he disclaimed fraternity with the children of the common Father of him and of all men; and justified by no duty but forbidden by every obligation, he even usurped power, in order to exclude forever from human fellowship millions, made by the same hand, after the same image with himself—both image and maker being God.¶

A vast number of the disowned were his brethren according to the flesh. The best blood of the caste he loved filled the veins of hundreds whom he discarded; and instances were not rare in which the Patriarchs of Slavery had not left enough of the blood of Africa to tinge the brow or to crisp the hair of their children, and Canaan, though sustained by the unsuborned testimony of Nature, was credited with the progeny of Shem upon the oath of Shem.¶

In his unnatural pride and hatred he abetted the wrath and cruelty of that portion of our race, which, beyond all others, exemplifies the degree to which it may be depraved; and to such wailing as agony never before extorted from human suffering, he not only turned a deaf ear but superadded injustice of his own adapted and intended to make the woe that caused it interminable and remediless.

As a Christian, he violated the standard doctrine of the church of which he was a professing member in one of its most important relations to humanity, and contemned its special admonitions touching the particular sin he committed. Of those whom he strove to degrade forever below the common level of mankind, and to strike from the roll of redemption, multitudes, belonging to and accepted by the same spiritual fellowship that

Back Cover

View in 2017 of Mt. Vernon Place, Baltimore,
where a statue of Taney was removed that year from this pedestal

ELI POUSSON/WIKIMEDIUM COMMONS

Made in the USA
Monee, IL
04 November 2026

67375704R00056